Leader's Guide for

Primary Source Readings in
World Religions

Leader's Guide for

Primary Source Readings in
World Religions

Patrick Tiernan

Saint Mary's Press®

I would like to thank my colleagues in the religious education department at Boston College High School, who walk with me as companions of Jesus. I would also like to acknowledge my teachers in interreligious studies: Thomas Casey, OSA; Kevin Dwyer, OSA; Francis Clooney, SJ; Roger Haight, SJ; Padraic O'Hare; Warren Kay; and Robert Neville. Your passion and commitment to dialogue continue to inspire my teaching. I need also to recognize my first teacher, John Vignol. As a scholar, mentor, and friend, your devotion inspired me to become a teacher. My parents, William and Barbara Tiernan, mean more to me than they will ever know, and I am eternally grateful for their witness of faith. My wife, Anitza, continually supported me during this project. She is my living sacrament of God's love. This book is dedicated to my students—past, present, and future. I am humbled to be called your teacher.

The publishing team included Steven McGlaun, development editor; Lorraine Kilmartin, reviewer; prepress and manufacturing coordinated by the production departments of Saint Mary's Press.

Shutterstock, cover image

Printed in the United States of America

1354

ISBN 978-0-88489-827-6

Contents

Introduction

Vision

> A just appraisal of other religious traditions normally presupposes close contact with them. This implies, besides theoretical knowledge, practical experience of interreligious dialogue with the followers of these traditions. Nevertheless, it is also true that a correct theological evaluation of these traditions, at least in general terms, is a necessary presupposition for interreligious dialogue. These traditions are to be approached with great sensitivity, on account of the spiritual and human values enshrined in them. They command our respect because over the centuries they have borne witness to the efforts to find answers "to those profound mysteries of the human condition" and have given expression to the religious experience and they continue to do so today.
>
> (Pontifical Council for Inter-Religious Dialogue, *Dialogue and Proclamation,* no. 14)

The preceding passage reflects the core values of this *Leader's Guide for Primary Source Readings in World Religions*. Studying world religions is an intellectual challenge coupled with an emotional endeavor to grow in sensitivity to the mystery of human nature. Teaching world religions requires an openness to new languages, cultures, and beliefs. By exploring the history of dialogue, students can begin to appreciate the unique contributions of each tradition without forgoing their own.

Young people raise many rich, yet complex, questions when reading about religious diversity for the first time. They may ask themselves: Why should I learn about other traditions when I still have to grow in my own faith? Are different religions simply different representations of the same reality? Can I be Roman Catholic and still study other rituals and beliefs? How can societies accept pluralism as an opportunity rather than an obstacle?

Creating a learning environment that is respectful, inquisitive, and genuine is essential to answering these inquiries. Bernard Lonergan, SJ, believed learning is the path to greater self-awareness, developed in four imperatives: be attentive to your perceptions of things so you may experience them accurately; be intelligent to learn about the entirety of an issue without focusing on its details; be reasonable by recognizing your limitations and the depth of what you are studying; and be responsible for bearing witness to truth on behalf of others. This philosophical framework may be adapted to prepare students for their experiences of other world religions.

Our Catholic tradition has a great deal to offer on these questions and more. The Catholic rule regarding other faith traditions is that we respect and admire them at all times. Although we Christians consider the grace and salvation of Jesus Christ as the norm, that consideration should not invalidate the cultural heritage and religious practices of others. Our vocation is found in experiencing the diversity of the world and the redemption that comes from truly loving our neighbors as ourselves.

Selection of Documents

One goal of *Primary Source Readings in World Religions* is to help students realize how different beliefs can contribute to a rich spiritual life. Additionally, we hope students will discover that the path to authentic dialogue requires commitment and sensitivity to others so the students' relationship with God may flourish. The readings chosen for *Primary Source Readings in World Religions* reflect these two goals.

Each chapter in the student book contains three readings, with the exception of the first and twelfth chapters. The first reading of each chapter is a primary text or scripture passage from a particular faith tradition. This reading has been selected to provide a firsthand experience of the creed of that tradition. The second and third readings come from other primary texts of that chapter's faith tradition, come from the writings of religious scholars, or are more biographical by reflecting the viewpoint of a modern practitioner.

The organizing principle of the student book is the pluralism of the religions themselves. Together their readings challenge the students to examine their own faith and the issues pertaining to world religions. Many of the readings are difficult, but with your help, the students can understand some of the great wisdom and guidance the global community has to offer.

The Leader's Guide

The leader's guide provides you with ideas to help your students explore world religions. For the students to complete the activities, you will need some materials, including large self-stick easel pads, small self-stick note pads, paper, and pens, pencils, or markers for each student. You will also need copies of various handouts throughout the chapters, enough for each student in your classroom. Look through the lessons before you teach them and gather the materials as needed.

This leader's guide provides various activities on a wide range of issues for the readings from the student book. Each chapter has a consistent structure, yet also provides variety in activities and techniques to help engage the students with the content of the readings.

Summaries

This leader's guide summarizes the reading selections to help you quickly identify readings that will be most helpful to your course.

Guiding the Students Through the Readings

The student book contains review questions that reinforce the students' basic understanding of the readings. The author believes the students might need more assistance while they read the texts, so he has provided ideas for guiding them through the readings in ways that keep learning largely in the students' own hands. Sometimes the author assigns portions of the readings to groups. Other times he provides additional questions on handouts for further reading and reflecting. Opportunities for "dialogue" with the author and for personal reflection are included to make the readings more relevant to the students. Once the students feel confident about the readings, they will be better able to discuss the implications and applications of the content through class discussion.

Going Deeper

After the activity that helps the students read the texts, the author addresses the readings in many different ways. The activities bring you a variety of teaching methods and discussion ideas for engaging your students in the material. The activities are student centered, often for groups or pairs, allowing you to encourage the learning process rather than direct it.

Prayer

Each chapter offers opportunities to pray with your students or to examine a meditation that relates to the world religion discussed in the chapter. Sometimes the author provides a spiritual reflection on the chapter readings. Other times he offers simple prayers or ideas for student-led prayer.

Action Ideas

The action ideas section gives you ideas for further research or action for the students. You might ask the students to pursue these suggestions with their families, either as additional homework or as opportunities to deepen their understanding of other religions.

Appendix

This book contains an appendix, "Additional Resources," to assist you in sharing the material with your students. The appendix suggests resources to help the students work through the material in each chapter.

An Invitation to Engage

Primary Source Readings in World Religions challenges your students to embrace the wisdom of the Church's teachings on other religions while growing in awareness of the pluralism in their world. Remind your students that their classmates bring a diversity of experience to these readings. The students will have strong feelings about issues of faith. Neither we nor our students necessarily know who identifies with which faith traditions, so it is a good general rule for us and our students always to speak with a spirit of respect and openness. A reminder about others' faith backgrounds invites us to reflect on our word choices and to be thoughtful listeners during our discussions.

Chapter 1

The Catholic Church and World Religions

Summaries of the Sources

Both readings in this chapter reflect the commitment of the Catholic Church to interreligious dialogue. Recognizing the common good in different faith traditions highlights the dignity we all share. Religious diversity should be a goal of—rather than an obstacle to—the global human community.

Declaration on the Relation of the Church to Non-Christian Religions (Nostra Aetate), by Pope Paul VI

Nostra Aetate, translated as "in our age," is a declaration from the Second Vatican Council that reflects the modern spirit during that important time in the life of the Church. Human nature is marked by essential questions that relate to our origins and purpose. Throughout history religions have had a way of permeating culture to raise these concerns. Catholicism is a monotheistic religion. It recognizes the one God of Judaism and Islam. These three religions are referred to as the Abrahamic faiths, because they identify themselves with the patriarchal lineage of ancient Israel beginning with Abraham. Other traditions such as Hinduism and Buddhism promote rites and practices that reflect different ways of finding truth through meditation or divine myths.

The central emphasis of *Nostra Aetate* is to address the charge of deicide (literally, "killing of a god") often leveled against the Jewish community. For centuries many people held a widespread perception that "the Jews" were responsible for the trial and Crucifixion of Jesus. The Church condemns this position and calls on the faithful to see the death of Christ as a symbol of God's love for all humanity.

The Church recognizes that goodness is found in all the faith traditions addressed in this document. People should honor this goodness through dialogue and mutual respect. The Church also upholds the need to confront discrimination or harassment based on religious differences. Therefore we should move beyond merely tolerating other faith traditions to focusing on the common call to unite as a global family. In appreciating the wisdom of other faiths, we can only grow and mature in our own.

"Meeting with Representatives of Other Religions: Address of His Holiness Benedict XVI"

In his first visit to the United States, in April 2008, Pope Benedict XVI met with a group of leaders representing various faiths from around the world. In his address the Pope explores the American dichotomy of church and state and how spiritual values can enrich public life. The Declaration of Independence notes that "life, liberty and the pursuit of happiness" are inalienable rights for all people. They reflect what it means to be made in the image and likeness of God, because we have free will and reason to reflect on our natures.

Freedom and religious diversity are intimately related. Pluralism is found in classrooms, at workplaces, and throughout local communities in America. This should give us pause to reflect on how we operate as a democratic society based on principles of justice and reason. Dialogue fosters our national identity through common ethical values and the call to live in solidarity with one another, enriched by the differences of our nation's people. Benedict XVI charges us with the responsibility of pursuing truth in all its manifestations, probing the ultimate foundation of all knowledge, which is found in the love of God's creative act.

Activities

Declaration on the Relation of the Church to Non-Christian Religions (Nostra Aetate), by Pope Paul VI

Guiding the Students Through the Reading

1. Assign the reading as homework and ask the students to note the main teaching of each paragraph.

2. As additional homework ask your students to create three columns with the following headings:
• What do I know?
• What do I think I know?
• What would I like to know?

Assign the students to brainstorm ideas for each tradition discussed—Hinduism, Buddhism, Islam, and Judaism.

3. During the next class period, have the students choose partners and share their homework responses. Use the following questions to guide the partners' discussions:
• Did the document teach anything new or surprising to you?
• What interests you most about studying world religions?
• What concerns do you have about approaching these faiths?

4. Invite pairs to share with the class what they discussed. Note understandings and questions the groups share.

"Meeting with Representatives of Other Religions: Address of His Holiness Benedict XVI"

Guiding the Students Through the Reading

1. Assign the reading as homework. Ask the students to find examples of religious language and images in the United States. For example, the public display of crosses on private land has evoked free speech debates, as has the issue of public school students' being required to recite the Pledge of Allegiance with its reference to God.

2. Remind the students about the First Amendment in the U.S. Constitution, which states, "Congress shall make no law respecting an establishment of religion, or prohibiting the free exercise thereof." Explain the two legal clauses regarding religion—establishment and exercise. The establishment clause limits the government's official support of any particular religious teaching in the public realm. The free exercise clause protects citizens from persecution or discrimination based on religious practices.

3. Divide the class into two groups. Inform the members of one group that they will represent the position in favor of allowing religious expression in public institutions (for example, teaching religion in a public school). Inform the other group members that they will represent the position opposed to religious expression. The two groups are to debate the following statement: The expression of religious language and its practices should be forbidden in public institutions in the United States.

4. Instruct the students that the debate will take a point-counterpoint format: each group will have the opportunity to speak five times—introduction of position, three supporting arguments in favor of their position, and a concluding argument that summarizes their stance and critiques the other group's position. The two groups should alternate speaking and should address the reasoning behind their argument while evaluating the opposing group.

5. Summarize the lesson by asking the students to explain the separation of church and state and the relationship of this principle to American politics and culture. Consider the following guiding questions:

- Can someone be both a faithful Catholic and an active citizen of the United States?
- Do religious beliefs have any place in the legislature?
- Could an atheist ever run for U.S. president?

Going Deeper

This activity involves researching religious pluralism by examining the phrase "*E pluribus unum*," which is the motto on the Great Seal of the United States. Latin for "out of many, one," this phrase may also be interpreted as a framework for understanding diversity. To introduce this activity, draw an analogy between interreligious dialogue and the classroom's diverse (or nondiverse) members.

1. Have the students document places of worship in their local communities or ask whether they know people in their neighborhoods who have different faith traditions from their own. Divide the class into groups of three to four. Ask the group members to share their experiences with one another.

2. In their groups have the students brainstorm challenges that may prevent us from learning more about religious diversity in our homes and schools.

The students may be reluctant to discuss this issue and may begin to think one tradition is better than another. Affirm that the readings from this chapter honor and respect the uniqueness of each tradition and the core values each embodies.

3. Ask the students to come back into the large group. Lead a discussion about how many faiths are represented in our cities and the larger American society.

4. Next have students return to their small groups. Ask the groups to explore ways this diversity would allow the diverse groups to become one, as the U.S. motto says. Which attitudes or behaviors would have to change for people to understand the cultural and religious diversity that makes up our country?

5. Allow each small group to present its findings. Ask the students in the large group to identify common themes found in the small groups' conclusions. Explain that exploring world religions allows the students to enrich their own faith while being open to the experiences and beliefs of others. To inquire about the history and practices of others makes us all more conscientious global citizens.

Prayer

1. Distribute copies of handout 1–A, "Sermon on the Mount of Intrareligious Dialogue," one for each student.

2. Ask one or two volunteers to read aloud the Sermon on the Mount from the Gospel of Matthew (5:1–12).

3. Next, invite several other volunteers to alternate reading from the handout, one paragraph at a time.

4. Ask the students to reflect on what they see as the central teaching points of the prayer on the handout. Invite them to share their responses.

Action Ideas

- Ask the students to brainstorm questions people ask when searching for greater meaning or significance in their lives. Have them explore how potential answers could initiate a dialogue across religious differences.
- Have the students survey the religious diversity at school. Invite them to explore the possibility of forming a religious diversity organization.

- Research the declaration *Dominus Iesus* from the Congregation for the Doctrine of Faith, found at the Vatican's Web site. What is the relationship between the universality of the Church and world religions? How does the Church understand the centrality of Jesus Christ?
- Explore the writings of the American theologian John Courtney Murray on religious liberty and how he envisions a nation grounded in the freedom of expression.

Sermon on the Mount of Intrareligious Dialogue

When you enter into an intrareligious dialogue, do not think beforehand what you have to believe.

When you *witness* to your faith, do not defend yourself or your vested interests, sacred as they may appear to you. Do like the birds in the skies: they sing and fly and do not defend their music or their beauty.

When you dialogue with somebody, look at your partner as a revelatory experience, as you would—and should—look at the lilies in the fields.

When you engage in intrareligious dialogue, try first to remove the beam in your own eye before removing the speck in the eye of your neighbor.

Blessed are you when you do not feel self-sufficient while being in dialogue.

Blessed are you when you trust the other because you trust in Me.

Blessed are you when you face misunderstandings from your own community or others for the sake of your fidelity to Truth.

Blessed are you when you do not give up your convictions, and yet you do not set them up as absolute norms.

Woe unto you, you theologians and academicians, when you dismiss what others say because you find it embarrassing or not sufficiently learned.

Woe unto you, you practitioners of religions, when you do not listen to the cries of the little ones.

Woe unto you, you religious authorities, because you prevent change and (re)conversion.

Woe unto you, religious people, because you monopolize religion and stifle the Spirit, which blows where and how she wills.

Chapter 2

Primal Religious Traditions

Summaries of the Sources

The origins of primal religions are not defined by a specific time, place, or figure. They are rooted in a spirituality committed to living in harmony with nature and all its inhabitants, in which the supernatural permeates everything. The myths and stories of traditional rituals in this chapter capture the extensive oral tradition that continues to the present day. In a sense the written word pales in comparison to the communal importance of storytelling and memory. To hear the spoken word is a virtue in itself.

Australian Aborigines: Excerpt from *Myths and Legends of the Australian Aboriginals:* "The Birth of the Butterflies"

First, this myth introduces symbolic imagery prevalent among primal traditions. The distinction between animals and humans is nearly nonexistent, as each assumes characteristics of the other. For example, the eagle-hawk and crow serve as authorities in the gathering of the creatures. In tribal communities elders often act on behalf of the people. Their wisdom is not questioned, because they have the gift of vision and prophecy. On one level this integration of animal and human signifies that all creation must work together to better the environment.

Second, death is not the conclusion of life but acts as a transition into another form of existence. The afterlife is symbolized by a new creation that assumes a different form. This is the beauty that the butterflies, once considered "ignorant and stupid," assume. Not only do physical properties change but also mental perceptions. The metamorphosis is a common figurative device in creation myths that represents how the essence of life remains despite assuming a new form.

Third, a cyclical view of time is a central theme. Time is not linear, with a definitive beginning and end. It is seasonal and follows the course of nature. Humanity should live in union with the changes that come from the natural world. Consequently, the afterlife is but another season to pass through.

Yoruba Creation Myth

This creation myth portrays the origins of life as the desire of the gods. The goodness of creation is seen through the deliberate preparation of the world—first the ground, then the sky and trees—to sustain human life. The created world was made specifically to ensure humans' viability.

One significant purpose of multiple deities is to show that each deity has its own function in the cosmos. For example, in this Yoruba myth, life, known as spirit or essence, is uniquely reserved for the supreme god Olodumare in the Yoruba tradition. This implies a mutual dependence between the created and creator, because everything has a place and purpose. Nothing in existence is without meaning.

The Lakota: Excerpt from *Lakota Woman:* "On the Ghost Dance," by Mary Crow Dog

To dance with the Spirit is a central rite of North American Indian nations such as the Lakota. Dancing celebrates the life that all beings experience. As an ecstatic movement, the Ghost Dance offers indigenous peoples the gift of visions to see beyond the pain of the present and the ability to become overwhelmed with spiritual fervor. The sacred hoop represents the notion of time reflected in the creation myths, where there is no beginning and no end. The hoop calls for an end to divisiveness and separation among different groups. The cycle of birth and rebirth is also apparent in the location of the Ghost Dance—"where this dance had been killed and where now it had to be resurrected."

The songs and rituals that Leonard Crow Dog learned from his father came from his father's father and so on. This cultural legacy is preserved through the memory of both pain and achievement. Customs are not solely followed out of a sense of obligation but also serve as an act of worship. To praise is to become empowered by the Spirit and to provoke that empowerment in others. Power here is not to be understood as domination, because that would imply using something for selfish gain. Instead, power is becoming more fully aware of our past and of the ancestors who gave rise to the present age.

Activities

Australian Aborigines: Excerpt from *Myths and Legends of the Australian Aboriginals*: "The Birth of the Butterflies"

Guiding the Students Through the Reading

1. Before assigning the reading, ask the students to write down examples of literature they have read with animals acting like humans or representing human characteristics. They should explain how the use of figurative language taught a moral or lesson. If your students have difficulty coming up with examples, you can mention Aesop's fables or George Orwell's *Animal Farm*.

2. Divide the class into four small groups. Ask them to share their examples with one another. Was learning by means of animal characters effective? Why or why not? How did childhood stories influence the students' upbringing?

3. Tell the students you will read them a story. Read aloud "The Birth of the Butterflies," asking them to pay close attention to the objects and characters in the myth.

4. When you have finished reading, write the following pairs of concepts on the board:

- oral/written
- animal/human
- conscious/nonliving
- existence/afterlife

Assign one pair of concepts to each group. Have the group members discuss whether they remember hearing those concepts in the reading. Tell them that primal traditions look at the two concepts as bridges rather than barriers. For example, where we may see a clear distinction between life and death, primal beliefs recognize them simply as different stages in life. Likewise, where we tend to see the world as human centered, Aborigines respect all creation equally.

5. Remind the students that myths often teach truths through allegories—extended metaphors in which the objects and characters are associated with meaning beyond the narrative.

6. Now invite the students to read the myth silently to themselves and to reconsider the concepts they discussed in their groups. Have them reflect on the following questions:

- How was your experience of the narrative different when you read it to yourself?
- Do you believe listening is a skill missing in our society today?
- Can reading a story by itself teach you truth?

7. Lead a large-group discussion about listening to a creation myth. Discuss how certain truths transcend the literary and cultural genres in which they are found. They are passed on from generation to generation and are a way of identifying oneself with one's ancestry.

Yoruba Creation Myth / The Lakota: "On the Ghost Dance," by Mary Crow Dog

Guiding the Students Through the Reading

1. Assign the readings as homework. Have the students write out any similarities or differences they find between the two readings.

2. Distribute copies of handout 2–A, "Creation and Ritual," one for each student. Have them answer the questions as they read the selections at home.

3. During the next class period, use the students' responses to continue discussing myths and the importance of rituals for a community.

Going Deeper

This activity offers an opportunity for the students to engage themselves with their immediate and extended family histories. They will create individual totem stories based on interviews with relatives. They will then present the stories to the other students.

1. Begin this activity by sharing the following background information with the students:

❖ Totem poles are indigenous to the Pacific Northwest region of North America. They symbolically represent a tribal or clan history's legacy and are "read" from the top to the bottom. They often portray animals associated with particular human attributes such as strength, courage, or wisdom. They serve as visible reminders of the past and present and are used for various purposes such as memorials or commemorations of important events. The raising and dedication of totem poles is accompanied by a great potlatch, a festival celebrating the community and the sharing of resources.

2. Show your students various depictions of totem poles and ask them to explain what story they think is being told. You may find images, links, and supplementary readings at the Museum of Archaeology and Ethnology at Simon Fraser University. You also can find a link at *www.smp.org*.

3. Ask your students to talk with their parents, grandparents, or other family members, taking notes to discover as much about their family histories as possible. Ask them to decide which symbols they will use to represent their family history. They should select four to six symbols. Remind the students that no text should appear in their totem histories. Encourage them to be creative in using images—personal pictures, graphic art, and so on.

4. After students have gathered their family histories, ask them to create a PowerPoint presentation of their images and narrative. If they cannot do a PowerPoint presentation, ask them to bring copies of the images they have selected. Ask them to discuss the following questions:
- What words come to mind for each image? Is the image significant for you or a family member?
- Describe how you decided which pictures you would use and which you wouldn't. Why do some visuals show an idea better than others?
- Would it have been easier simply to write a report on your family history? Why or why not?
- Was representing something personal in a public setting difficult? Explain.

5. Divide the class into small groups of four or five. Have them briefly share with one another their responses to the questions in step 4. Have the students attempt to understand one another's totem histories before making their own presentations. Were there common representations of family births or marriages? of other significant events or people?

6. Conclude by explaining to the students that some indigenous terms from nations of the

Pacific Northwest and from groups elsewhere have become colloquial phrases, as opposed to the authentic values they embody. *Totem pole*, *pow-wow*, and *taboo* are examples of tribal language we often use as generalizations to inaccurately represent rituals and practices not our own. For example, "She's higher up on the totem pole," "Let's have a pow-wow," and "That's a taboo issue" are all ways we corrupt the sacredness of indigenous culture. Have the students discuss ways they can break down these stereotypes and learn more about the true meanings and origins of the sacred rites of indigenous peoples.

Prayer

Call the students to prayer by asking them to explain what we celebrate at the Eucharist. Remind them that *eucharist* means "thanksgiving." It is both a symbolic reminder of the Last Supper and an invitation for us to enter into communion with the Body and Blood of Jesus Christ.

1. Ask the students to reflect on traditions they may remember or observe during the Thanksgiving holiday. What does it mean to be thankful for something or someone?

2. Distribute copies of handout 2–B, "Black Elk Speaks," one for each student. Remind students of the historical period in which Chief Black Elk of the Lakota nation lived. Although conflict occurred between native Americans and western settlers in the nineteenth century, there are many parallels between Lakota spirituality and mainline Christianity.

3. Read the Thanksgiving prayer aloud together as a class. You may want to mention that this was a personal family prayer that Black Elk's daughter Lucy (Black Elk) Looks Twice recited from memory. You may offer the following questions:
- What does this prayer remind you of from the readings in this chapter?

- Why is calling the Great Spirit "Grandfather" significant?
- How does the image of family appear in Black Elk's prayer?

Action Ideas

Encourage your students to learn more about indigenous traditions and their histories, using the following ideas:
- Have your students explore indigenous traditions' relationship between ecological justice and respect for nature.
- Invite your students to research different native American nations and their cultures and rituals.
- Show your class the documentary *The World of American Indian Dance,* about the art of native American dance. What concepts do the students see reflected in the video?
- Read other creation myths to your students so they can cultivate the practice of mindful listening.

Creation and Ritual

Answer the following questions from your reading of the Yoruba Creation Myth and "On the Ghost Dance":

1. What is the significance of Olodumare and Obatalá's creating the world over several days?

2. The Yoruba creation myth concludes with Olodumare dispersing his divine power to the other deities. Obatalá, in turn, endows humans with divine power. What does this tell the Yoruba people about their purpose in the world and their connection to their deities?

3. What is the role of song and music in the revival of the Ghost Dance?

4. How does memory influence the movement of the Spirit for the Lakota Nation?

5. Explain in your own words the relationship between creation myths and rituals. How do rituals commemorate creation?

"Black Elk Speaks"

I am talking to you, Grandfather Great Spirit, on this day.
Pitifully, I sit here.
I am speaking for my relatives, my children,
    my grandchildren, and all my
    relatives—wherever they might be.
Hear me, Grandfather, Great Spirit.

With your help, our needs are taken care of.
You have helped us in the time of want during the past.
And on this day we wish to thank you.
Hear me, O Great Spirit.
This day is a day of thanksgiving.
The nations of living things the world
    over—and we the two-leggeds, along with the
    children and the smaller ones with them—come
    to you today to express thanks.

In the future, make us see again a red day of good.
In the past, you have preserved us from evil
    on this red road.
Keep us on this road, and do not let us see anything wrong.

I, my children, and my grandchildren shall
    walk—led like children by your hand.
You have helped us in all things.
And Grandfather, Great Spirit, through your power
    alone we have survived.

Grandfather, Great Spirit, you have come and
    put us down—gathered together on mother earth.
And while we continue in this world, you provide food for all living creatures.
So we give you thanks on this day.
Grandfather,
Take pity on me.

One day, we shall go and arrive at the end of the road.
In the future, we shall be without any sin
    at all.
And so it will be in the same manner for my
grandchildren and relatives who will follow as well.
We give you thanks, Grandfather, Great Spirit.
I am sending this prayer to you.

(The prayer on this handout is from *Black Elk: Holy Man of the Oglala*, by Michael F. Steltenkamp [Norman, OK:
University of Oklahoma Press, 1993], pages 118–119. Copyright © 1993 by the University of Oklahoma Press.
Used with permission of the University of Oklahoma Press.)

Chapter 3

Hinduism

Summaries of the Sources

Hinduism affirms that proper religious practice requires physical and mental discipline. In seeking the truth that God is love, the believer encounters various ways to express the divine reality. This expresses Hinduism's polytheistic beliefs, in which the number of deities reflects the diverse and relational dimension of Brahman, or the essence of reality. Hinduism asserts that our duty in life is to look beyond the illusion of materialism and be liberated from the cycle of existence.

Excerpts from *The Bhagavad-Gita:* The Second and Third Teachings

These selections from *The Bhagavad-Gita* reflect many of the central teachings of Hindu philosophy. The dialogue is between the great warrior Arjuna and Krishna, an avatar (embodiment) of the deity Vishnu. The point is that our obligations in life may require us to perform actions that appear to contradict our senses. The world provides us superficial means to acquire happiness, such as wealth and power. They are finite and limited. To be authentic beings, we must accept the transitory nature of our existence and seek what is eternal. The selections address the following major points:

- **Impermanence.** All humans go through a series of changes over their lifetimes—birth, adolescence, and adulthood. We may feel certain emotions and feelings, but these do not define our existence. They are transitory and mask the essence of reality. Change is a key feature of this world. In accepting change we grow in the courage to face what is truly real.

- **Reincarnation.** An essential aspect of the Hindu worldview recognizes our bodies as vessels that constantly change based on how we fulfill our duties to one another. We should not fear death, because it is a part of the great cycle of birth and rebirth, in which we continue to develop our spiritual natures.

- **Desire.** Wealth, power, and pleasure are common goals people struggle to attain. People suffer when these goals are taken away or withheld. A central belief of Hinduism holds that physical desires should be engaged fully so we may discover their limited natures.

- **Duty.** We have to meet our civil and divine obligations to better our reincarnated lives. Our responsibilities are found in the relationships we develop with family, friends, and God. These responsibilities often conflict with one another. When we place the needs of others before our own, we mature in the ability to serve the wider human community.

Stories of Vedanta Sages: Excerpt from *Philosophies of India:* Teachings on *Maya,* by Heinrich Zimmer

The concept of *maya* is an abstract philosophical concept that speaks to the illusory nature of this world. False or limited perceptions that we only wish were genuine are often mistaken for what is truly real. *Maya* entails not only physical objects, such as people or animals, but also feelings, such as joy or anger. They are real because people perceive them to be. In these narratives from Śaṅkara, we find that ignorance prevents us from seeing true reality. We are anxious about potential dangers in our surroundings that limit our ability to meet the needs of our immediate communities. Perception is belief—we often see what we choose to believe. Wisdom requires us to listen to the voice of God before we speak. Because everything participates in the divine reality, we should not be selective in what we see and with whom we associate. All created life deserves our respect.

Excerpt from *All Men Are Brothers: Life and Thoughts of Mahatma Gandhi as Told in His Own Words,* compiled and edited by Krishna Kripalani

The autobiographical reflections of Mohandas Gandhi (*mahatma* is a title of respect, like *sir* or *reverend*) demonstrate that personal faith can be enriched when it is open to the experiences of religious teachings that are not our own. As imperfect beings we have an imperfect understanding of religion. Gandhi uses the metaphor of a tree to symbolize the one and true perfect religion (the trunk) and how it passes through several manifestations of doctrines (branches and leaves). Being religious is not a separate trait of our lives but is integral to the activities of community life such as politics. Building the Reign of God must begin with everyday behaviors that model how it has "already, but not yet" been completed in this lifetime. Truth is paramount in our journey to discover the creation of God. Often individual truths are mistaken for the one Truth that is the nature of God. Language limits our ability to grasp this divine reality. Gandhi uses a syllogism (a logical relationship of ideas) to express this simple yet profound belief—God is Truth, Truth is Love, and therefore, God is Love. This love is realized in our relationships with others. Our actions should be oriented to what is of ultimate concern, namely, discerning the inexhaustible nature of God.

Activities

Excerpts from *The Bhagavad-Gita:* The Second and Third Teachings

Guiding the Students Through the Readings

1. Ask the students to read the selections as homework. Distribute copies of handout 3–A, "Examining *The Bhagavad-Gita*," one for each student. Ask the students to complete the handout as they read.

2. During the next class period, discuss student responses. When discussing their answers, make sure the students have understood the main points of the reading. The students should be able to identify and explain the following points:

- Although our modern culture may promote living an excessive lifestyle, Hinduism recognizes that genuine happiness can occur only when we transcend these limited pleasures and desire to know truth.
- Self-control is a virtue of the mind and body. Arjuna is a model of how human nature is divided between what we know and what we believe we know. Killing represents a metaphor for overcoming ignorance and tempering our senses to attain knowledge of God.

Stories of Vedanta Sages: Excerpt from *Philosophies of India:* Teachings on *Maya,* by Heinrich Zimmer / Excerpt from *All Men Are Brothers: Life and Thoughts of Mahatma Gandhi as Told in His Own Words,* compiled and edited by Krishna Kripalani

Guiding the Students Through the Readings

1. Ask the students to read both selections as homework. As they read ask them to take notes about insights they gain and questions they have about the readings. For the next class period, assign the students to bring in images from newspapers or magazines that reflect examples of "perceptions" and "truths" the popular media promote. For example, what do the media promote as the things you need to be successful? to be happy?

2. Designate two areas in the classroom to represent positive and negative examples of perceptions and truths the students selected. Have them tape their pictures in the corner that best describes their images. Ask the students to say why they felt their images were positive or negative. What experiences contributed to this belief? What would be required for this perception or truth to change or be modified?

3. Have the students survey the various posted images. Ask volunteers to summarize what the images mean to them. Were there duplicates, and what might that mean? Is there an emotion one may feel by looking at these? If so, what is it and why would someone experience that feeling?

4. Discuss the following:
❖ Why are some cultural images more appealing than others?

❖ How do these images represent the concept of *maya*?

❖ What myths or images need to be revealed or broken to see the love of God present in the world?

❖ Can two people perceive the same image as both positive and negative? Why or why not?

5. Conclude by noting that the search for truth unites human beings. Perceptions of what is true may vary based on experiences and education. Poll the students about what they found to be the most difficult and insightful aspects of the readings. Recognize that the students may conclude that truth is relative— that what makes something real is merely people's belief in it. Remind the students that divine revelation does not disclose all reality at once but instead reveals glimpses of the one Truth that Gandhi recognizes in the different religious traditions.

Going Deeper

This activity requires some background reading from another Hindu narrative. The *Ramayana* is the story of Rama, who is another avatar of the deity Vishnu. In Indian mythology he is the paradigm of proper action and the model of virtuous living. His journey to become king of Ayodhya is plagued by betrayal and exile. His consort, Sita (herself an avatar of the goddess Lakshmi), is abducted by the demon Ravana. Rama must seek the aid of Hanuman, the monkey god, to confront the evil army. He is successful and returns to his kingdom, where he is crowned. You may find brief and extensive summaries of this poetic narrative on several Web sites. Links are provided at *www.smp.org*.

1. Distribute copies of handout 3–B, "Understanding *Ashrama, Dharma,* and *Moksha,*" one for each student. Ask the students to study the handout definitions of these three central concepts. Have them write a one-page reflection that addresses how the concepts relate to the readings in this chapter. Have them choose partners and share their reflections with each other.

2. On the board write the following three questions that encapsulate the Hindu worldview:
• Who am I?
• What should I do?
• Whom will I become?

Remind the students that "Who am I?" refers to *ashrama,* "What should I do?" refers to *dharma,* and "Whom will I become?" refers to *moksha.* You may also want to share that the Hindu teaching on reincarnation allows for an undisturbed meditation on a person's identity, because it will evolve over multiple lifetimes.

3. Ask the students to reflect on their stage of life (adolescence), moral behaviors (virtue and sin), and identity (relationships). How have they changed since childhood, and how will they change in adulthood? You may want to share a personal story about your own growth and development and how one's identity is shaped by the tension between first, what one *wants to* become and whom one *wants to* associate with, and second, what one *should* become and whom one *should* associate with. The dynamic of free will versus determinism is a theme found throughout Hindu literature.

Prayer

This prayer offers an activity in comparative theology with two hymns in praise of Deví and Mary, two female paradigms of the Hindu and Christian traditions. The first is the *Saundarya Lahari*, an ecstatic tribute to the goddess attributed to the eighth-century Hindu theologian Śaṅkara. *Saundarya Lahari* means a "flood of beauty" and refers to the aesthetic experience of her beauty. The second is the *Stabat Mater,* a medieval meditation on Mary's presence at the death of Jesus. The Latin phrase means "the mother was standing." It is in sharp contrast to the Hindu hymn in emphasizing the grief and pain over Mary's beloved Son's suffering and death.

   1. Distribute copies of handout 3–C, "Hymns of Bliss and Sorrow," one for each student. Ask the students to read the verses from the *Saundarya Lahari* to themselves, reflecting on the descriptions of Deví and her works.

   2. As a group, read aloud the *Stabat Mater* and conclude with the *Memorare*:

> Remember, most loving Virgin Mary,
> never was it heard
> that anyone who turned to you for help
> was left unaided.
>
> Inspired by this confidence,
> though burdened by my sins,
> I run to your protection
> for you are my mother.
>
> Mother of the Word of God,
> do not despise my words of pleading
> but be merciful and hear my prayer.
> Amen.

   3. Conclude by asking the students how the emotions in both hymns could relate to each other. Guide discussion by asking the following questions:

   ❖ Who am I? What difference would it make if these hymns were sung rather than read?

   ❖ What image of humanity do you see in both hymns?

You may want to share the following to provide some context for the prayers:

• The Blessed Mother and the goddess Deví differ on several levels. Mary is ever virgin in the Catholic tradition, whereas Deví is sexually active and married to God (Shiva, spelled Śiva in the reading). Spiritual devotion to Deví results in immediate joy for the worshiper, whereas faithful devotion to Mary represents a point where suffering is necessary for the joy that exists after death. Yet both hymns embody the spiritual and physical divide through feminine imagery. Both require meditation to see beyond the visual of Deví's bliss and Mary's sorrow. Moreover, the reader is invited to contemplate the mystery of human nature through the power of two women who stand in solidarity with the male deity but affirm their own identities through a particular vision of transcendent hope.

Action Ideas

Invite the students to learn more about the historical and cultural dimensions of Hinduism through the following activities:

• Find artistic representations of Hindu deities.

• Research the prejudice and discrimination that the members of the "untouchable" class face in modern India.

• Look into the purpose of *puja,* the elements necessary for its practice, and the different forms it can assume.

• Research more deeply the philosophical tenets of nonviolent resistance that Gandhi promoted during British imperialism and how it may be developed in American diplomacy.

Examining *The Bhagavad-Gita*

The story of Arjuna's struggle to fight in war is a metaphor for human existence and the obstacles we humans face in discovering our true natures. Use the following questions to guide your reading of *The Bhagavad-Gita*:

1. In referring to people who give in to worldly desires, Lord Krishna explains, "Driven by desire, they strive after heaven / and contrive to win powers and delights / . . . Obsessed with powers and delights, / their reason lost in words, / they do not find in contemplation / this understanding of inner resolve." How could this be seen as a warning to Arjuna?

2. Based on these selections, how is the battlefield a metaphor for human existence?

3. In Hinduism why is death something not to be feared?

4. What duty or obligations must Arjuna fulfill?

5. Summarize the ideas behind the Second and Third Teachings in your own words.

Understanding *Ashrama, Dharma,* and *Moksha*

Ashrama refers to the four stages of life. The first stage is that of a student, where the goal is to acquire knowledge and build moral character. The second stage is that of a householder, which begins with marriage and recognizes service to family and the deities. The third stage begins when one's children become adults and an individual enters the ascetic stage by withdrawing from society and begins to focus on meditation and the reading of scriptures. The final stage is that of a *sannyasin,* where one renounces the materialism of the world.

Dharma expresses the concept of duty all must abide by. Karma represents the actions we perform that either fulfill or contradict our *dharma.* Duty is rooted in one's social place *(ashrama)* despite karma, which may promote selfish behavior. Moral consistency is an attribute of proper *dharma,* where good actions beget good consequences for an individual.

Moksha explains how liberation from suffering can be attained by fulfilling one's duty and obligations *(dharma),* prescribed by one's place in life *(ashrama).* This struggle is represented by the wheel of *samsára,* and its justice is found in humanity's ability to overcome this cycle.

Hymns of Bliss and Sorrow

Saundarya Lahari

Your beauty is such,
O daughter of the snow-capped mountain,
That the foremost poets, Viriñci and others,
Strain to match it in some way,
And so too immortal maidens
Eager to see You
Travel by their minds
Along the path to union with the mountain Lord
So hard to attain just by asceticism. (12)

Whoever contemplates You in his heart,
O essence of ambrosia,
Abundant and radiant like an image carved in moonstone,
Will quell the pride of serpents
As if he were the king of birds,
He will cure those afflicted by fever
With the streaming nectar that showers from his glance. (20)

Prayer—my foolish words;
Sculpture—all my hand gestures;
Circumambulation—my going about;
Mode of obligation—my eating and so on;
Deep reverence—my lying down;
Dedication of self—my complete happiness:
Whatever of mine shines forth—let it all be the same as worship of You. (27)

Eternal one,
Some people with a taste for great, uninterrupted pleasure
Place the triad "memory," "womb," and "flourishing"
Before Your mantra and worship You
With rosaries strung with jewels that grant desires,
They offer hundreds of obligations,
Streams of butter from the cow Surabhi
Flowing onto the fire of Śiva. (33)

You are mind, You are air,
You are wind and the rider of wind,
You are water, You are earth,
Beyond You as You evolve

There is nothing higher,
There is only You, and
When You transform Yourself by every form,
Then you take the form of consciousness and bliss
As a way of being,
O Śiva's youthful one! (35)

Illumining the sun with small flames,
Bathing the moon whence nectar flows with drops from moonstones,
Satisfying the ocean with its own drops of water—
And me too,
Prasing You with Your own words,
O Mother of all words. (100)

The *Stabat Mater*

The sorrowful mother was standing in tears
Near the cross as her Son was hanging there, and
Through her sighing soul
That shared His sadness and was sorrowing
A sword pierced. (1)

O how sad and afflicted
Was the blessed mother of the only-begotten,
As she was bewailing and sorrowing and trembling,
As she stood looking upon
The punishments of her renowned Son. (2)

O mother, font of love,
Make me feel the force of sorrow,
That I might lament with you,
Make my heart burn in loving Christ, God,
That I might be pleasing to Him. (5)

Make me truly weep with you,
Sorrowing with the crucified as long as I live;
To stand near the cross with you,
To be with you willingly, wailing—
This I desire. (7)

Virgin famous among virgins,
Be not bitter toward me now, but
Make me wail with you,

Make me carry the death of Christ,
A share in His passion
As I recollect His wounds. (8)

Make me
Guarded by the cross,
Protected by the death of Christ,
Cherished by grace, and
When this body dies,
Make it that my soul be given the glory of paradise.
Amen. (10)

Chapter 4

Buddhism

Summaries of the Sources

Because Buddhism stems from the belief that suffering is intimately related to life, this chapter's readings highlight the methods and practices in Buddhism that lead to liberation from this state. They explore how the enlightened self must focus on the teachings of the Buddha, the support of the community, and the expectations of morality. The readings explain how happiness comes from detaching ourselves from mental and physical desires.

Excerpts from *The Dhammapada*

The practice of being mindful is paramount to understanding Buddhism. When we are mindful, the Buddha teaches, we awaken from our ignorant perceptions about what is real and true. Just as dreaming can deceive us into thinking we have accomplished something or have possessed an object, so does the physical world entrap our minds and bodies into desiring inanimate things. This constant state of wanting creates pain in our lives, because we are never satisfied. In the selections from *The Dhammapada*, we are told that authentic freedom comes from the ability to behave and contemplate in complete awareness of our surroundings. It requires that we are physically, mentally, and spiritually present to the people and places around us.

Wisdom comes from the efforts of individuals to know where they are ignorant and to learn from sagacious people. Because Buddhism teaches there is no permanent self, it is futile to say something is mine or yours, because there is no ego to claim objects in this world. In letting go of those things most precious to us, we learn to appreciate all reality and its inherent goodness. This insight comes from taking refuge in the community and meditating on the teachings of the Buddha. Through this, one realizes that transcending the suffering of this world is possible.

Zen Buddhism: Excerpt from "The Platform Sutra of the Sixth Patriarch"

This narrative depicts the "sudden enlightenment" school of thought in the Zen tradition. It shows how the desire to become enlightened can itself become an illusion. For Hui-neng enlightenment comes suddenly, like lightning from a clear sky when the Fifth Patriarch teaches him the *Diamond Scripture*. He does not marvel over the verses he has written but instead returns to work as usual. Enlightened beings must work so others can find their own true natures. This is an essential part of community living—to teach others how to discover themselves. Zen masters often use *koan*s, or logic riddles, to teach this to their disciples. A well-known *koan* is "What is the sound of one hand clapping?" *Koan*s are intended to clear the mind and to serve as objects of meditation. They are not meant to have a direct answer or solution.

The practice of meditation serves this goal by removing the psychological obstacles that prevent us from reflecting on our true natures. Its purpose is to return us to a pure state of mind, free from false beliefs and perceptions. When we possess internal calm, the external world of change and uncertainty comes into focus. Meditation not only is the physical act of contemplation but also directs us to sustain a calm state of mind throughout our lives.

Tibetan Buddhism: Excerpt from *Freedom in Exile: The Autobiography of the Dalai Lama,* by Tenzin Gyatso

In this excerpt Tenzin Gyatso, the thirteenth dalai lama, describes the intricate process of finding the next Dalai Lama. He reflects on what outsiders may consider to be a strange method of finding the next great Buddhist teacher. The doctrine of reincarnation is not merely a metaphysical explanation of how one reality is transformed in another lifetime. Its essence is found in a person's willingness to serve all conscious beings in whatever capacity is most needed. It shows that the teachings of the Buddha are inexhaustible and may require multiple manifestations for humanity to learn the right path to liberation.

In the same way that the title *Dalai Lama* translates as "ocean of compassion," so is his role as leader of Tibetan Buddhism to show others the true meaning of human existence—to love and serve others in their fullest expressions. Our task is to cultivate an appreciation for all creation without using it for selfish purposes. The Dalai Lama reminds us that to understand the truth that resides in world religions, we must grow in our awareness of their rituals and traditions.

Activities

Excerpts from *The Dhammapada*

Guiding the Students Through the Readings

1. Assign the selections from *The Dhammapada* as homework. Distribute copies of handout 4–A, "Interpreting *The Dhammapada*," one for each student. Have the students fill in the sentence starters on the handout as they read.

2. Begin the next class session by discussing the reading and handout with the class. You can use the following questions for discussion:

❖ What did you find most interesting in the reading?

❖ What did you find confusing?

❖ How did the reading help you in completing the sentences on the handout?

❖ What sentences on the handout were the easiest to answer? the most difficult?

3. Divide the class into three groups, one for each chapter in the excerpts. Ask the groups to compare this style of writing to others they have experienced in other classes. Ask what they find most confusing or enlightening about the Buddha's teachings. Remind students that they must first assess where their own ideas are before properly understanding the central ideas of Buddhism. Because Buddhism is often described as a philosophy rather than a religion, the students should remember that the quest for wisdom is a practical task first and an intellectual exercise second.

Zen Buddhism: Excerpt from "The Platform Sutra of the Sixth Patriarch" / Tibetan Buddhism: Excerpt from *Freedom in Exile: The Autobiography of the Dalai Lama,* by Tenzin Gyatso

Guiding the Students Through the Readings

1. Divide the class into two groups. Assign one group to read and summarize the passage from "The Platform Sutra of the Sixth Patriarch" by paying attention to the characteristics essential to being a good student or disciple. Have the other group read and summarize the passage from Tenzin Gyatso, the Dalai Lama, by paying attention to which characteristics are essential to being a good teacher or leader.

2. Ask the groups to use the following questions to guide their summaries:

- ❖ What are my primary responsibilities in the role of student or teacher?

- ❖ What obligations do I have to others?

- ❖ How can I develop better traits for my role?

- ❖ How can self-discipline improve my awareness of mental obstacles?

3. Lead a large-group discussion. Ask the students to comment on the nature of the teacher-student relationship, using the following questions:

- ❖ How is each role responsible to the other?

- ❖ What ensures that the relationship flourishes?

- ❖ How can discipline be a positive experience for a student or disciple?

4. Continue the discussion by explaining that both leaders and disciples have the power to shape each other's growth and development. Note the mental and physical exertion required for authentic students or teachers to find their true potential.

Going Deeper

Use this activity as an opportunity to explore the central tenets of the Four Noble Truths and the steps in the Noble Eightfold Path.

1. Distribute copies of handout 4–B, "The Path to Nirvana," one for each student. Ask the students to read it silently to themselves.

2. When the students have finished reading, share the following with the class:

- ❖ The Buddha is often referred to as the great physician, because he diagnosed the human condition. The Buddha's main concern was to eliminate suffering and to find a cure for the pain of existence. Like a physician he observed the symptoms—the disease that humanity was suffering from. Next he gave a diagnosis—the cause of the disease. Then he gave the

prognosis—it was curable. Finally he gave the prescription—the method to cure it. This process embodies the Four Noble Truths. The path to nirvana, or liberation from suffering, is known as the Noble Eightfold Path.

The path to nirvana (a word meaning "to extinguish desire") follows a similar line of reasoning in which we must learn to correct our perspectives and behaviors. We must realign our false actions with right ones. For example, when we say something derogatory about someone or some group of people, we should develop "right speech." This means we learn that language has a proper time and place and should not be used for selfish purposes.

3. Ask the students for examples of obstacles that prevent us from following the Buddha's advice to remove suffering from our lives and to develop right behaviors and attitudes. The students may ask whether following the Buddha's teachings is sacrilegious. Point out that Buddhism teaches similar ethical principles to Christianity and that our treatment of others is the most common and fundamental dimension that all world religions share.

Prayer

Invite the students to create their own prayer service to reflect on how desire leads to suffering in the world. Ask them to select a Scripture reading (e.g., Luke 12:13–21 or Ecclesiastes 5:10–11) and an image from popular culture (television, music, or literature) that summarizes the limited nature of material possessions. Divide the class into groups based on similar readings or images. Then discuss why certain images are more prevalent than others. You can also introduce a comparative analysis by seeing where the Old Testament or New Testament addresses the redemptive nature of suffering.

Action Ideas

- Raise awareness about the connection between social justice and meditation. Two recent documentaries examine how prisoners participated in the Vipassana—a physically and emotionally challenging ten-day Buddhist retreat. Two films—*The Dhamma Brothers* and *Doing Time, Doing Vipassana*—explain how human nature is capable of change.

- Challenge your students to keep a "gratitude journal" for a week. Ask them to write daily reflections on experiences and encounters for which they are grateful, regardless of whether the experiences seemed positive or negative. Invite the students to share how living in a constant state of mindfulness affects their personalities or relationships with others.

- Have your students research the similarities and differences among the three divisions of Buddhism—Theravada, Mahayana, and Vajrayana. Ask them to reflect on which concept in each they found the most appealing and the most difficult.

- Ask your students to learn more about how different cultures have interpreted the teachings of Gautama the Buddha.

- Show your students pictures or clips of mandalas and ask them to research the Buddhist doctrines these symbols help explain.

Interpreting *The Dhammapada*

In *The Dhammapada* Gautama the Buddha supports the essential teachings of Buddhist philosophy. They focus on redirecting the mind to grow in awareness and releasing false perceptions and desires. Use the following sentence starters to brainstorm how you understand awareness, desire, and emotions:

1. I am most calm when . . .

2. I am most childish when . . .

3. I am least aware of my surroundings and acquaintances when . . .

4. The clearest memory I have of my childhood is . . .

5. True knowledge occurs when . . .

6. Pride is harmful if . . .

7. Wisdom can be found in . . .

8. The people I associate with are . . .

9. My strongest desire has caused me pain by . . .

10. When I am in distress or pain, I take refuge in . . .

The Path to Nirvana

The Four Noble Truths represent the teachings of the Buddha on the nature of human existence and the hope that may come from meditating on it. The Noble Eightfold Path represents the proper balance of the mind and body in harmony with each other. This series of actions is known as karma. An individual may require several lifetimes to achieve nirvana.

The Four Noble Truths

1. Life is suffering. To live means to suffer, because human nature is not perfect and neither is the world we live in. During our lifetimes, we have to endure physical suffering such as sickness, old age, and eventually death. We also have to endure psychological suffering like sadness, disappointment, and depression. Although there are different degrees of suffering and there are also positive experiences in life that we perceive as the opposite of suffering, such as ease, comfort, and happiness, life in its totality is imperfect and incomplete, because our world is subject to impermanence.

2. Suffering comes from attachment. The origin of suffering is attachment to material things and ignorance of how our mind is attached to impermanent things. The reasons for suffering are desire, passion, and prestige—constant craving and clinging. Because the objects of our desire are transient, their loss is inevitable. Thus suffering will necessarily follow. An example of this is the idea of a "self," which is a delusion, because there is no abiding self. We are merely a part of the ceaseless process of the universe.

3. The end of suffering is attainable. The third noble truth expresses the idea that suffering can be ended by attaining disinterest. This means human actions can overcome suffering simply by removing the cause of suffering. Attaining and perfecting disinterest is a process of many levels that ultimately results in the state of nirvana. Nirvana means freedom from all worries, troubles, complexes, fabrications, and ideas. It is not comprehensible for those who have not attained it.

4. The Noble Eightfold Path leads to the end of suffering. The gradual path of self-improvement is described in detail as the Noble Eightfold Path. It is the middle way between the two extremes of self-indulgent hedonism and excessive self-depriving asceticism. It leads to the end of the cycle of rebirth. Craving, ignorance, and their effects will gradually disappear, as progress is made on the path.

The Noble Eightfold Path (Wisdom / Ethics / Psyche)

1. Right view is the cognitive aspect of wisdom, to see the true nature of all things.

2. Right intention is the first step toward compassion. It represents a commitment to forming a good will and attitude toward all life.

3. Right speech is to refrain from false rumors and insults and to speak positively toward everyone. It recognizes that one should speak only when necessary.

4. Right action refers to the proper use of one's body and to respect for others' bodies. Life is to be honored and respected and should manifest itself in moral relationships.

5. Right livelihood means we should earn a respectable living in line with how we speak and act. We should not engage in immoral activities that corrupt our good natures.

6. Right effort is required for all other steps in the path. It calls for self-discipline and control over all activities in life.

7. Right mindfulness focuses on the proper balance of bodily efforts and mental dispositions. Being mindful means maintaining a contemplative state of mind that remains in a continual state of gratitude.

8. Right concentration is the primary focus of meditation, which intensifies with the alignment of the other steps. It is a state in which all mental faculties are directed onto a central focus.

Chapter 5

Sikhism

Summaries of the Sources

A commitment to meet the spiritual and material needs of others characterizes Sikhism. Based on an egalitarian philosophy, it seeks to create equality among men and women, students and teachers, masters and disciples. It emphasizes religious faith as a personal relationship with the divine order, requiring meditation and contemplation to distinguish between material wants and spiritual needs. By honoring the teaching legacy of the ten historical gurus, Sikhs live a life of service to the community.

Excerpt from *Textual Sources for the Study of Sikhism*

This passage details the deeds and insights of Guru Nanak emphasize the biographical nature of Sikhism's founder. Where other religions stress the importance of ritual or doctrine, Sikhs' first affirmation of faith is the lineage of the ten gurus. To know the teachings of these wise men is to know the social equality this religion—one of the ten largest in the world—preaches.

From the moment of Guru Nanak's birth, we find auspicious signs of a moral leader and prophet—"that time of fragrant peace" when "celestial music resounded in heaven." These supernatural signs are important to bear in mind, because they point to a natural event. "Baba" Nanak models true discipleship by learning what is required of him and then questioning the very method in which it is taught. He becomes the teacher while still a student. Study without contemplation is devoid of spiritual insight. Nanak gives his blessing by humbly teaching the ignorant. Moreover, without feeling the need for praise, he gives to the needy. Even while working he is regarded as "remarkably conscientious," a trait that embodies the Sikh ethic of what may be seen as servant leadership.

The episode that describes his preaching retells an important narrative for understanding the social and cultural position of Sikhism in the world. By saying "there is neither Hindu nor Muslim," Guru Nanak affirms the beliefs of each tradition while denying that either is central. Sikhism affirms an egalitarian morality beyond class that originates with a communal call to fellowship and service. Doctrinal differences may lead to division, but all humanity can identify with the call to live peacefully. Both Hinduism and Islam claim Guru Nanak as their own, yet he taught that we belong to one another first.

Guru Nanak's travels with Mardana underscore a concept familiar to many Eastern faith traditions—karma. Karma refers to the actions in our lives that perpetuate either good or evil among others. By refusing to satisfy Mardana's basic need of water, Vali Qandhari focuses on Mardana's superficial appearance and is unable to see the humanity underneath. The significance is not that Guru Nanak is able to produce water from the ground but rather that the reservoir of Vali Qandhari disappears. It symbolizes the karmic reaction of what happens when we do not tend to the needs of our human family. When we give to others, we are provided with abundance.

Excerpts from The *Japji*, the Sikh Morning Prayer

The place of *Japji* in the Sikh tradition is an invaluable one, because it combines worship and meditation. As the *Japji* states, it is intended to be chanted. A mantra is a sacred word, prayer, or belief that is repeated continually. The *Mūl Mantra* is explained by the subsequent meditations. These sayings establish a contemplative commentary that Sikhs chant both as a form of devotion and as a reflection on the teachings of the gurus.

This selection reveals the rich theological discourse of the Sikh tradition. The *Japjî* teaches the traditional monotheistic creed of oneness and unity throughout all creation while emphasizing the polytheistic teaching on reincarnation. The greatness of the Supreme or Eternal One is tempered by the inability to describe the affinity that exists between the temporal and divine. There is a sense of utter dependence made hopeful by a wealth of grace. The Word is transcendent and beyond our comprehension, and yet we desire to know and love what it teaches. Through listening, one is liberated from the mental and physical hardships of reality.

Excerpt from *The Self Spirit,* by Wadhawa Singh

This autobiographical selection by Wadhawa Singh can be characterized as a discourse on the metaphysics of Sikhism. Metaphysics is the branch of philosophy dealing primarily with the nature of reality. Metaphysics also seeks to explain the reality of an object based on how people perceive or understand it.

The question Wadhawa Singh's grandson poses reflects an awareness that few individuals entertain: What is the nature of the spirit, and how can I recognize it? Here we see the answer in the form of a relationship, the *Aatma-Parmatma,* which is the individual contemplation of the divine essence of the world. It is similar to the Hindu experience. We learn that by simply closing our eyes, we can focus on our consciousness and watch our attention to the physical fade. There are degrees of consciousness as there are degrees of awareness. Some people are enlightened beyond this world, while others resist the path to truth. When Wadhawa Singh invites his grandson to imagine visiting India—despite

the other grandchildren believing he is "really" in California—he teaches that we must lose ourselves in the unconscious depths of our minds while letting go of the emotional strains that hinder our spiritual development. In purifying our thoughts and removing what we perceive, we begin to learn divine knowledge, which is eternal.

Activities

Excerpt from *Textual Sources for the Study of Sikhism*

Guiding the Students Through the Reading

1. Assign the reading as homework. Then distribute copies of handout 5–A, "Knowing Guru Nanak," one for each student. Ask the students to complete the handout individually as they read.

2. Begin the next class period by asking the students to brainstorm religious biographies they know or have heard of. You may initiate the discussion by raising the following questions:

❖ Can you understand a faith tradition through personal stories?

❖ Do biographies allow readers to witness a more human dimension of religion?

❖ What difference, if any, does it make if a religion has a historical founder?

3. In a large-group discussion, have students share their understandings of the reading. What stood out for them? Did anything seem familiar? Is it significant that Sikhism is just a little more than five hundred years old?

Excerpts from The *Japjî,* the Sikh Morning Prayer / Excerpt from *The Self Spirit,* by Wadhawa Singh

Guiding the Students Through the Readings

1. Assign the readings as homework. Have the students write answers to the following question as they read:

- What is the association between our physical bodies and our spiritual natures?

2. During the next class period, stick two sheets from a self-adhesive easel pad on opposite walls of the classroom. At the top of one, write, "What the readings said about our physical bodies is . . ." On the other write, "What the readings said about our spiritual natures is . . ."

3. Have the students find a partner. Ask them to share with each other their reactions to the homework question. Then two at a time, one at each easel pad sheet, invite the students to write brief answers to the sentence starters.

4. After all the students have shared with their partners and written their answers on the easels, read the answers to yourself. Then summarize aloud your findings. You may want to read one or two student comments. Offer your own reflections that the mind-body relationship can be abstract at times but that understanding it is imperative to understanding many of the great religious traditions in our world.

5. Next, distribute copies of handout 5–B, "Exploring the 'Five K's' of Sikhism," one for each student. Ask the students to read it silently. As they read have them reflect on the following and give you their first impressions:

- ❖ What makes these five K's essential to being a good Sikh?

- ❖ How does each K answer the guiding question in this assignment, What is the association between our physical bodies and spiritual natures?

Either you may place the students into five groups and have them respond to the question, or you can lead a large-group discussion to explain and summarize the handout.

Going Deeper

The readings in this chapter highlight the unique place of Sikhism among other religions. Challenge the students to reflect on the nature of religions and how they adapt to different beliefs while developing an original faith tradition.

Moreoever, symbolism fulfills an important role in Sikh practices and may be misconstrued if students are not familiar with Sikhism's theological and historical roots. Use this opportunity to explore ways to understand religious imagery.

1. In small groups, have the students brainstorm what makes a religion monotheistic or polytheistic. Direct them to develop a definition of monotheism and polytheism, identify examples of monotheistic and polytheistic religions, and list traits of monotheism and polytheism.

2. Ask the students to identify examples of Hindu and Islamic teachings. If students are not yet familiar with these traditions, you may omit this instruction or simply ask the students to identify what they would consider to be monotheistic or polytheistic beliefs.

3. Next ask students how they see Sikhism integrating monotheistic and polytheistic characteristics. What evidence can they find to support their claims? Note that although Sikhism is regarded as monotheistic, the influence of Hinduism and its understanding of the universe is prevalent in its writings.

4. Show the students an image of the Sikh symbol the Khanda. Explain that like all symbols, it can be interpreted literally and figuratively. The literal understanding could connote violence or aggression. The symbolic understanding explains a reality beyond our capability. The Khanda itself, a double-edged sword, is placed in the center to signify the destruction of ignorance and the divine reign of the Supreme One. The two swords on the left and right stand for political and divine rule. The circle in the center is known as a Chakra, an iron weapon that symbolizes the timeless and infinite nature of the divine and the unity of all human beings.

5. Summarize the discussion by noting how the contemporary media sometimes falsely associate violence with religious practices, thus contributing to negative stereotypes. Remind the students that many world religions teach that although self-defense may be necessary on rare occasions, the respect for life must be upheld at all times.

Prayer

This prayer is an example of a hymn used in Sikh wedding rituals. It is called the Lavan. It literally means "circling" and symbolizes the union of two people entering the ultimate union with the divine. Each circle represents higher levels of existence, in which the couple becomes completely absorbed into the divine reality.

1. Distribute copies of handout 5–C, "The Marriage Lavan," one for each student. Ask the students to read the hymn to themselves. Have them identify Sikh beliefs in the stanzas of the prayer.

2. Hold a large-group discussion about the nature of marriage. How is it both a literal and a metaphorical commitment? What preparation is required to enter into such a union? How might the Sikh and Christian theologies of marriage be similar in this respect?

Action Ideas

- Research the historical lineage of the gurus and how they maintained the teachings of Guru Nanak. Will there be another guru? What is the contemporary state of Sikhism in the world?
- Explore the Hindu influences on the Sikh faith tradition. How can one call Sikhism more egalitarian or communal based than Hinduism?
- Explain the origins and meaning of the turban. Have students explore the relationship between clothing and spirituality.

Knowing Guru Nanak

1. What is the significance of Baba Nanak's having "deep and mysterious thoughts" while resolving everyone's doubts and questions? How might such a spiritual prodigy be seen today?

2. How is Nanak's work at the commissariat a summary of the Sikh faith?

3. What Christian parables remind us of the encounter with Vali Qandhari? On the other hand, why is it important to be cautious when comparing stories from different religions?

4. In one sentence summarize the meaning to Sikhs of Nanak's death.

Exploring the "Five K's" of Sikhism

The following five terms describe the ideal Sikh disciple who is baptized in the tradition. Guru Gobind Singh—the tenth and last historical guru of Sikhism—formally established the K's. Stress the importance of maintaining physical purity as a path to spiritual knowledge.

1. **Kesh** refers to having uncut hair and represents the natural will of God. Its preservation is a commitment to the teachings of Guru Nanak. **Reflection:** How are our bodies a temple for the Spirit of God?

2. **Kangha** is a comb that keeps hair neat and tidy. It is a mark of discipline for the Sikh and symbolizes hygiene and spiritual purity. **Reflection:** How do we maintain our relationship with God?

3. **Kara,** a steel bracelet, is to be worn as a reminder to act morally. It is a call to act dutifully and honorably toward others. **Reflection:** What reminds us of our duty to others?

4. **Kachh** refers to soldier shorts that serve to remind Sikhs to be chaste and exercise self-restraint. **Reflection:** How can bodily desires prevent us from gaining spiritual wisdom?

5. **Kirpan,** a sword, stands for self-reliance and dignity. It is purely symbolic and not meant to be used. It symbolizes spiritual power in one's life. **Reflection:** What are the most important values for us to live by?

The Marriage Lavan

Creator, as we revolve in the first divine circle,
 We resolve to return to the world of action.
As we resolve to act rightfully, and make Your
 Word
 Our god and scripture, our misdeeds are
 dispelled.
Scriptures steadfastly urge us to act righteously
 And contemplate Your Name.
By remembering the True Guru,
 All our misdeeds and offences are
 dispelled.
Bliss is ours at once, we are blessed with great
 fortune,
 And the Divine tastes so very sweet.
Nanak the slave says, in the first circle
 The wedding ceremony is begun.

In the second circle,
 We meet the True Guru, the Primal Being.
By the fear of the Fearless One,
 Our self gets rid of the filthy ego.
In pure awe of the Divine, we sing praise day
 and night,
 And we see the Divine present
 everywhere.
Infinite in all directions,
 intimate in everyone,
Within and without, there is only the One.
 Joining the faithful, we sing songs of joy.
Nanak the slave says, in the second circle
 The soundless Word begins to play.

In the third circle,
 The bliss of detachment fills the mind.
By joining the faithful, we join the
 Transcendent One.
 We are blessed.
We attain the Immaculate One, we worship
 the One
 With praise, and we recite the Word.
By joining the faithful, we join the Blessed
 One.

We tell the untellable story.
Our heart begins to beat with the divine
 melody.
 We recite the name with fortune glowing
 bright on our foreheads.
Nanak the slave says, in the third circle
 The Divine One rises in our detached
 mind.

In the fourth circle,
 We find equanimity, we unite with the
 Divine One.
Through the Guru, we naturally become one
 with the One,
 Body and mind exult in delicious joy.
But we taste the sweetness only if we please
That One,
 By meditating day and night.
My Guide, all my desires are fulfilled;
 Through the divine Name, felicitations
 ring.
The Sovereign's blessing completes the
 wedding rite;
 And the bride is in bliss with the Name in
 her heart.
Nanak the slave says, in the fourth circle
 The imperishable Groom is wed.

(The Sikh wedding hymn on this handout is
from *The Name of My Beloved: Verses of the
Sikh Gurus*, translated by Nikky-Guninder
Kaur Singh [New York: HarperCollins
Publishers, 1995], pages 147–148. Copyright
© 1995 by Nikky-Guninder Kaur Singh.
Used with permission of the author.)

Chapter 6

Confucianism

Summaries of the Sources

The dignity of the individual requires that proper rituals be practiced in society. Confucianism advocates a relational ethic that recognizes the importance of family, community, and government in developing the individual. Cultivating virtue in accordance with tradition is essential for humanity. Learning for the sake of learning is a central dimension of this belief. By treating others as we desire to be treated, we model the proper goodness in our natures.

Excerpts from *The Analects,* by Confucius

Virtue is a benevolent action that allows people to reflect on how they may improve their ways of life. Confucius promoted a view of life that aligned itself with the needs of the community. Community members are inextricably related to one another. Proper social behavior does not pursue self-interests but rather continually upholds the needs of the immediate family and extends to the broader human community.

The Analects are a collection of Confucius's teachings that his pupils gathered. They provide simple, yet profound, insights into the human condition. The selections focus on the following ideals:

- **Relationships.** The five principal relationships are the cornerstone of Confucianism. Rulers must govern judiciously. Parents must prepare children to be moral citizens. Siblings must promote harmony in the home. Spouses must be loyal to each other. Friends must foster compassion.

- **Benevolence.** This is the supreme virtue—to treat others as one wishes to be treated. It maintains that empathy allows one to fully enter into the experience of others and allows for genuine compassion. Goodness is realized in how it is applied consistently to all members of society.

- **Ritual.** Contrary to understanding tradition as merely commemorating an event on an anniversary or special occasion, ritual is the sustained reflection on all aspects of behavior—speech, listening, and action. Rituals should inform everyday actions and serve as the basis for how we interact with everything from the familiar to the unknown.

- **Learning.** We should not seek education simply because it allows us to attain other goods such as a career or financial opportunities. Instead learning should become a spiritual investment for an individual and should create a sense of urgency to know more. Knowing more does not mean merely learning about multiple subjects. It is also about the degree to which we know about something. It is a matter of depth, not breadth.

"The Great Learning"

Order is necessary for peace and tranquility to occupy our world. By ignoring order we focus inward and strive to develop ourselves in competition with others. The Way of learning recognizes that individuals should nurture the principle of identification. We identify ourselves with the self but must move to the family. We identify ourselves with the family but must move to the state. We identify ourselves with the state but must move to the nation. We identify ourselves with the nation but must move to humanity. This identification begins with the individual but concludes that our ultimate "self" can be found only in the wider human family.

Confucian ethics require that if a community desires a particular virtue or behavior among its members, the right actions must be put into place. This is demonstrated in the wording of the great leaning that for a goal to be accomplished, one should be aware of the beginnings and ends of things. We must situate ourselves in the legacy of tradition and strive to further its influence on social norms. Social disorder occurs when this process is not followed, whereas harmony arises when it is.

Excerpt from *Confucius: The Secular as Sacred,* by Herbert Fingarette

Herbert Fingarette highlights the dignity of the individual in Confucian philosophy by using the image of a vessel. He ponders how an adorned container is precious, asking, "Whence does its sacredness come?" (p. 75). If social propriety requires us to act respectfully at all times, we must look beyond the superficial characteristics of human actions. We are more than biological creatures and, consequently, should behave with greater sensitivity to the needs of society. Our power comes from acting out of respect for the rituals society has set forth. Our sacredness stems from how we stand in relation to others.

Virtues should transform individuals to act properly in social situations. We should have suitable preparation and cultivation of behaviors, just as the vessel is molded and formed in a proper ceremony. When humanity flourishes, it reflects the goodness we show one another. Ideal people can suspend their egos, dismiss their pride, and focus on how to properly forge other holy vessels.

Activities

Excerpts from *The Analects,* by Confucius

Guiding the Students Through the Reading

1. Assign the selections from *The Analects* as homework. As additional homework, ask the students to choose four of Confucius's sayings they find most significant. Have them summarize each saying.

Remind the students of the centrality of the Five Relationships to Confucius—ruler-subject, parent-child, spouse-spouse, older sibling-younger sibling, friend-friend. Tell the students they will use the passages they selected as a framework for reflecting on their place in Chinese thought.

2. During the next class period, divide the class into five small groups. Assign each group one of the Confucian relationships mentioned in step 1 and have them reflect on the following questions:

❖ What is the most challenging part of this relationship?

❖ Which rituals are associated with this relationship?

❖ How do culture and media influence our views of this relationship?

❖ Does the relationship have other social bonds not emphasized in Confucianism?

Each group should assign one member to serve as a recorder for the group responses.

3. Have the groups pass around their reflections so all the students have a chance to read about and discuss the other four relationships. After each group has read and discussed the other four groups' reflections, ask for volunteers to summarize one of the group responses other than their own.

4. Designate five spaces in the classroom for each relationship. Each space should be large enough for several students to stand.

Invite the students to stand in the space for the relationship they feel is most important for establishing social harmony. Ask the students to explain their reasoning and to provide an example. After a few volunteers have spoken, allow the students to move around the room based on what they heard. For those who changed, ask how they were convinced.

"The Great Learning" / Excerpt from *Confucius: The Secular as Sacred,* by Herbert Fingarette

Guiding the Students Through the Readings

1. Assign the readings as homework. Ask the students to reflect on the purpose of education. Is it to prepare for higher learning? obtain a steady job? gain financial security?

2. Have the students find partners. Have the pairs discuss the connection between academic learning and social learning. Do they see a difference between the classroom and the "real world"? If so, where do they learn how to behave in certain social situations?

3. Distribute copies of handout 6–A, "The Proper Rite," one for each student. Have the students complete it with their partners. Invite the pairs to create one more scenario for the class to consider.

4. As homework invite the students to bring home the handout and ask a parent or another adult to respond to the situations. Were the adults' answers similar to the students'?

5. During the next class period, ask the students to talk about their responses to the handout, the scenario they created with their partners, and the way their parent (or other adult) reacted to the situations on the handout.

Going Deeper

This activity provides an opportunity to research the historical context of Confucius's social ethic and the contending philosophies that provided the background for his call to govern justly and love appropriately.

1. Share the following with the students:
❖ Social or legal philosophy is often a response to the cultural issues of a given time and place. It is not usually developed by itself but serves as an alternative perspective, usually in times of conflict or strife. The context of Confucius's thoughts is no different. He wrote and taught during a time in China's history when states were at war. Leaders either stressed discipline over morality or believed universal acceptance of all people would solve the social ills of the country. Confucius's writings represent a balance between these two extremes. His approach is commonly referred to by one of the central books in the Confucian canon, "The Doctrine of the Mean."

2. Distribute copies of handout 6–B, "'The Doctrine of the Mean,'" one for each student. Ask the students to read it silently. Then have them answer the following questions:
❖ What Confucian terms and ideas do you see reflected in the reading?

❖ Why might the balance of a middle position be necessary in our world today?

❖ What would this mean look like in education?

❖ How would it look in government or friendship?

3. Next, explain the beliefs of the two ideologies of the Confucian era that influenced his teachings—legalism and mohism.
• The legalists believed that human nature required a strict government to enforce rules and discipline to establish social order. Only one relationship was necessary, namely that of the ruler and subject. If the ruler led sternly, the subject would act properly.

- Mohists, on the other hand, believed that the unconditional love of humanity could replace any need for punishment. People are innately good, and this is a sufficient social principle for society to thrive.

4. Conduct a large-group discussion, asking the following questions:

❖ As a follower of Confucianism, how would you know when you had achieved the mean of social behavior?

❖ Where do you see elements of legalism and mohism in Confucius's teachings? How is his thought different from these viewpoints?

❖ If Confucius visited America in the twenty-first century, what recommendations would he make to improve its government, culture, and society?

❖ Do you think Confucianism is a religion or an ethic? Explain.

5. Summarize the discussion by mentioning how social change does not occur immediately. To learn new rites and practices requires time and patience. The path to social harmony challenges the global community to put aside distinctions such as nationality and to identify with our true family—humanity.

Prayer

The concept of prayer is elusive in the Confucian tradition. This is not to say that Confucianism does not understand worship but rather that formal petitionary prayers readers may be familiar with were not present in many Chinese writings.

1. Distribute copies of handout 6–C, "Xunzi on Heaven," one for each student. Note that the excerpt is from Xunzi (third century BC), a Confucian philosopher who emphasized education in many of his writings. This is what may be called a negative prayer— it reflects what Xunzi believed was *not* the proper focus of prayer. Though rituals were necessary for virtuous living, he emphasized the need to distinguish between the earthly and heavenly realms. Ask the students to find partners. Have the pairs read the prayer aloud together.

2. Ask the students how Xunzi's description of heaven differs from their understandings. Based solely on this reading, how would they define prayer and its role in the Confucian tradition? Do they see any connection with the excerpts from "The Doctrine of the Mean"?

Action Ideas

Encourage the students to learn more about the nature of relationships and the proper cultivation of virtuous behavior, using these suggestions:

- Talk with a local or state legislative representative about the obstacles facing laws that promote the needs of neighboring communities.
- Interview a parent, grandparent, aunt, uncle, or other elder family member about how he or she sees respect in the home and how it contributes to making better citizens. Ask what the person sees as essential to the proper formation of children.
- Create a poll for your school that asks what the defining characteristics of true friendship are. Discuss common themes that emerge from the responses.
- Research various forms of government, including democracy, socialism, fascism, plutocracy, and theocracy. What are the strengths and limitations of each? How do they balance the dignity of the individual with the needs of society?
- Explore the role of the visual and performing arts in Confucianism, in particular calligraphy and music *(wen)*.
- Study the influence of Mencius on Chinese thought. Write a formal report describing how he was faithful to tradition while elaborating on the goodness of human nature.

The Proper Rite

For each of the following social situations, identify the following:
- how people would tend to respond
- an example of an inappropriate action
- the appropriate Confucian response

    1. Attending a wedding or social celebration:

    2. Learning a subject in which you have little interest:

    3. Seeing a friend who has lost a loved one:

    4. Being introduced to someone for the first time:

    5. Communicating with an older relative:

    6. Write another scenario with your partner:

"The Doctrine of the Mean"

What Heaven has conferred is called The Nature; an accordance with this nature is called The Path of duty; the regulation of this path is called Instruction.

There is nothing more visible than what is secret, and nothing more manifest than what is minute. Therefore the superior man is watchful over himself, when he is alone.

"The superior man's embodying the course of the Mean is because he is a superior man, and so always maintains the Mean. The mean man's acting contrary to the course of the Mean is because he is a mean man, and has no caution."

The Master said, "Perfect is the virtue which is according to the Mean! Rare have they long been among the people, who could practice it!

The Master said, "I know how it is that the path of the Mean is not walked in: The knowing go beyond it, and the stupid do not come up to it. I know how it is that the path of the Mean is not understood: The men of talents and virtue go beyond it, and the worthless do not come up to it.

"When one cultivates to the utmost the principles of his nature, and exercises them on the principle of reciprocity, he is not far from the path. What you do not like when done to yourself, do not do to others.

In a high situation, he does not treat with contempt his inferiors. In a low situation, he does not court the favor of his superiors. He rectifies himself, and seeks for nothing from others, so that he has no dissatisfactions. He does not murmur against Heaven, nor grumble against men.

"Benevolence is the characteristic element of humanity, and the great exercise of it is in loving relatives. Righteousness is the accordance of actions with what is right, and the great exercise of it is in honoring the worthy. The decreasing measures of the love due to relatives, and the steps in the honor due to the worthy, are produced by the principle of propriety.

"The duties of universal obligation are five and the virtues wherewith they are practiced are three. The duties are those between sovereign and minister, between father and son, between husband and wife, between elder brother and younger, and those belonging to the intercourse of friends. Those five are the duties of universal obligation. Knowledge, magnanimity, and energy, these three, are the virtues universally binding. And the means by which they carry the duties into practice is singleness.

Therefore, the superior man honors his virtuous nature, and maintains constant inquiry and study, seeking to carry it out to its breadth and greatness, so as to omit none of the more exquisite and minute points which it embraces, and to raise it to its greatest height and brilliancy, so as to pursue the course of the Mean. He cherishes his old knowledge, and is continually acquiring new. He exerts an honest, generous earnestness, in the esteem and practice of all propriety.

(The material on this handout is from *The Doctrine of the Mean*, by Confucius, translated by James Legge [Oxford, England: Clarendon Press, 1893], at *www.sacred-texts.com/cfu/conf3.htm*, accessed October 13, 2008.)

Xunzi on Heaven

Constant principles underlie Heaven's behavior. Heaven does not prevail because you are the sage Yao or disappear because you are the tyrant Jie. Blessings result when you respond to Heaven by creating order; misfortune results when you respond to it with disorder. When you concentrate on agriculture and industry and are frugal in expenditures, Heaven cannot impoverish your state. When you store provisions and act quickly in emergencies, Heaven cannot afflict illness on your people. When you are singleminded in your cultivation of the Way, Heaven cannot send disasters. Thus, even if they come, droughts and floods will not bring starvation, extremes of temperature will not bring illness, uncanny phenomena will not prove unlucky.

On the other hand, if you ignore agriculture and industry and spend extravagantly, then heaven cannot make your country rich. If you are negligent concerning provisions and slow to respond to cries, Heaven cannot keep your country whole. If you renounce the Way and act recklessly, Heaven cannot make you lucky. In such a case, starvation will result even without flood or drought; illness will occur even without severe weather; misfortunes will occur without any uncanny phenomena. Even though the seasons are identical to those of an orderly age, the resulting fortune or misfortune is different. But you should not resent Heaven. It is your Way that is responsible. Thus those who can distinguish what is in the realm of Heaven and what is in the realm of man are men of the highest order . . .

Are order and disorder the product of Heaven? I say, the sun and the moon, the stars and the constellations are the same as they were in the time of Yu and Jie. Yu brought order, Jie created disorder, so order and disorder do not come from Heaven. Are they a product of the seasons? I say, plants sprout and grow in spring and summer, and are harvested and stored in fall and winter, just the way they were during the reigns of Yu and Jie. Yet Yu brought order, Jie disorder, so order and disorder are not the product of seasons. Is it land then? I say, obtaining land leads to life, losing it leads to death, just as in the time of Yu and Jie. Yet Yu brought order, Jie disorder, so order and disorder are not a product of land . . .

Why does it rain after a prayer for rain? I say, for no reason. It is the same as raining when you had not prayed. When there is an eclipse of the sun or moon, you "save" it; when there is a drought, you pray for rain; when an important decision is to be made, you divine. It is not that you can get anything by doing so. It is just decoration. Hence, the gentlemen considers them ornament, but the common people think spirits are involved. To consider them ornament is auspicious; to consider them as spiritual acts is inauspicious.

(The material on this handout is from *Chinese Civilization: A Sourcebook*, second edition, revised, edited by Patricia Buckley Ebrey [New York: The Free Press, a division of Macmillan, 1993], page 24. Copyright © 1993 by Patricia Buckley Ebrey. Reprinted with permission of The Free Press, a division of Simon and Schuster, Inc.)

Chapter 7

Taoism

Summaries of the Sources

The Taoist readings in this chapter highlight the need to act in harmony with nature. The Way is simply known as the Tao, and it is relative to each individual who seeks to know. Ignorance comes from the inability to look beyond dualisms in the world, such as good and evil, happy and sad, healthy and ill. Paradoxes can be seen as logical contradictions, but Taoism uses them to explore human nature and the way attachments of the mind and body lead to an imbalance in the order of the universe.

Excerpts from *The Way of Lao Tzu (Tao Te Ching),* translated by Wing-Tsit Chan

These chapters capture the essence of Taoist principles. They are teachings from the first teacher of Taoism, Lao Tzu, for individuals to meditate on and practice daily. In them he promotes the doctrine of *wu-wei,* which is the ability to achieve without exerting force. In yielding to nature, one finds peace. This can be applied to how governments officiate, teachers educate, and students learn. True ability is recognized by the ease with which it is demonstrated.

The sage is the epitome of this characteristic. He is one who does not need to boast or speak excessively. The authentic teacher is one who allows students to cultivate their own learning. The genuine philanthropist does not seek recognition. The sage contributes to the betterment of everyone and does not ask for anything in return.

The symbol of the yin-yang reveals the teaching that weakness overcomes strength and that by not acting, we are, in fact, acting. The symbol is a circle with one dark half with a white circle inside it and a white half with a dark circle inside it. Yin is the dark half, the passive and subtle cosmic element of nature. Yang is the white half, the active and forceful cosmic element of nature. Each element resides in the other (represented by the small circle), to show the interconnectedness of the two facets of nature. We must adapt to new discoveries and be flexible in our goals.

Excerpts from *Chuang Tzu: Basic Writings,* translated by Burton Watson

The Way has an ineffable nature. It cannot be named or described. We should understand this idea not as an abstract belief but rather as a reflection on the limitations of our ability to describe things. Language can often complicate complex issues more than enlighten them. In this reading Chuang Tzu, who is often referred to as the second teacher of Taoism, uses the idea of dreaming to explain how we should be more aware of the wonder and beauty in all creation. The butterfly symbolizes the need for a metamorphosis, a radical change of mind for individuals who remain stagnant in their thinking.

Likewise the story of the older woman emphasizes the need to look beyond appearances and embrace all of life. When we accept defeat as graciously as victory, the paradoxes of life resolve themselves. We must learn to let go of controlling our actions and allow the world the chance to guide us.

Excerpt from *The Taoist Body,* by Kristofer Schipper

This passage from Kristofer Schipper underscores an interesting point in the discussion of how religion is defined. He recognizes that if Taoism is to be understood as a set of doctrines and dogmatic creeds, then it faces an uncertain future in how it is to be practiced. Chinese teachings and narratives have greatly influenced its history, which requires a closer examination from Western scholars. Schipper asserts in *The Taoist Body* that "the very notion of religion as we define it in the west is an obstacle, and a great number of observers have fallen into the trap of failing to see that in a society so dissimilar from ours the religious system must also be very different" (p. 2). Difference prevents us from engaging in a dialogue with traditions that, we may prematurely conclude, have nothing to contribute to our own faith tradition. Because a society is unlike ours, we may assume we have nothing to gain from studying its history. In defining religion we limit its ability to speak to all humanity and relegate its significance to historical events and cultural time lines. Because Taoism is not bound to time or language, it can adapt itself to any of the Western traditions.

Activities

Excerpts from *The Way of Lao Tzu (Tao Te Ching),* translated by Wing-Tsit Chan

Guiding the Students Through the Readings

1. Assign the readings as homework. Ask the students to reflect on chapter 78 in particular. Distribute copies of handout 7–A, "What Does Lao Tzu Mean?," one for each student. The students should consider in the text and on the handout the analogy between water and human nature.

2. During the next class period, divide the class into groups of four. Assign to each group one of the human applications of water from the handout. One student in each group should serve as a recorder, another should draw a symbol or image for the group's application, and the other two should brainstorm three to five examples of how to practice the application.

3. Ask the students in each group to post their symbols or images around the classroom. Invite the individual students to walk around and examine each depiction, noting which application they think each picture explains. Have volunteers explain why they associate certain principles with the pictures.

4. Ask the groups to share their ideas about acting on the principles. They should propose concrete examples other students can relate to. For example, "A way to practice the first principle, 'Do not be arrogant or overambitious,' is to show your appreciation to family and friends who have played a role in your success at school."

5. Have other students comment on the examples and reflect on what obstacles might prevent a community (such as the family, school, or nation) from practicing the concept of nonaction in everyday life.

6. Conclude the lesson with some comments about putting Taoist principles into action, focusing on these or similar words:

- ❖ Instead of thinking that behaving in a Taoist manner contradicts the Catholic faith, consider how acting like this is flexible to adapt itself to any religious tradition and may allow us to reflect more deeply on the sacramental life of the Church.
- ❖ Become aware of how society acts in a rigid or limiting manner that prevents full participation from all its members.

Excerpts from *Chuang Tzu: Basic Writings,* translated by Burton Watson / Excerpt from *The Taoist Body,* by Kristofer Schipper

Guiding the Students Through the Readings

1. Before assigning these readings as homework or classwork, have the students share their understanding of religion. Have them write a brief response to the following questions:

❖ How do you define religion?

❖ Has your perception of religion changed over the years?

❖ What part of religion do you tend to disagree with or remain confused about?

❖ Do you consider yourself to be religious or spiritual? Is there a difference in the terms we use to speak about faith?

Assign the readings as homework.

2. During the next class period, have the students choose partners and share their responses about religion, noting differences and commonalities. How would a Taoist sage respond to the questions? Is it simpler to perceive religion as a way of life than as an institution?

3. Have the partners recall the image of a butterfly Chuang Tzu uses to explain the growth and development required for true wisdom. Invite the students to construct time lines of their lives. Have the line extend from birth at one end to the present day at the other. On the line the students should mark where significant changes have occurred and write a brief description. Ask them to consider why these people or events were fundamental to their growth as individuals.

4. Have the students consider when they thought a positive or negative image or experience influenced their personalities. You may suggest that even negative experiences may have a positive effect on who they are today. Also have them consider challenges they anticipate encountering in the immediate future. Ask them to explore ways they can remain open to growth and change throughout their lives.

Going Deeper

This activity involves reflecting on the nature of the yin-yang symbol as a way of resolving conflict and competing emotions.

1. Begin by telling the students our lives contain many dualisms: joy and sadness, hot and cold, right and wrong, first and last, love and hate. What gives us peace is when these apparent opposites dissolve and we see things as they truly are. We have been socialized to embrace one and reject the other. But this also causes distress, because we continually fear we will lose that which we see as good and we intentionally avoid that which we see as bad.

2. Tell the students there will be times where what we see as bad is in fact good and where what we see as good is bad. This is not being flippant but reflects the reality of our world and our relationships. For example, being accepted into the college of your choice will not necessarily bring happiness, because you may have to leave your family and friends.

3. Post a picture of the yin-yang at the front of the classroom. Give the students a minute simply to focus on the image. After they are done, have them turn to another student and comment on what they saw. Did they associate the yin and yang with any particular emotions or characteristics? Did they identify themselves with a part of the image?

4. Next ask them to write a three- to five-sentence reflection describing how they see duality in their lives. As an extended assignment, ask them to compare the philosophies of Taoism and Confucianism as representing the yin and the yang, respectively.

This is a common comparison among the Chinese religions.

5. Conclude by commenting that to Western minds, celebrating failure or smiling when we are sad seems illogical. The Taoist mentality affirms that by letting go of our emotions and desires, we gain control of them. Just when we experience joy, we realize that sadness will eventually follow. When we suffer the pain of hunger, we eat to be satisfied and then suffer again from feeling full. This is what the "eye" in both the yin and the yang embody—there is no such thing as a pure emotion or feeling. Sometimes being still and focused is all that is needed to find wisdom.

Prayer

Taoist prayer is synonymous with meditation. For this activity invite the students to participate in a walking meditation. This can be more difficult than it appears. Find an open space in school or prepare to take your class outside if weather permits.

Distribute copies of handout 7–B, "Walking Meditation," one for each student. Remind the students to be aware of their every thought, breath, and action when reading and performing this activity. They should know that meditation does not require complete silence, nor does it require them to stop everything to do it. Meditation simply couples our breathing with our ability to reflect. It is a perpetual state of mindfulness. Allow 10 to 20 minutes for the meditation. Then invite the students to reflect on their experiences.

❖ What was most difficult about this activity?

❖ How could you practice meditation daily?

Action Ideas

Research the Book of Changes—the *I Ching*. Explore the relativity of values and the role it plays in living day to day, reflecting on how our existence is perpetually in flux.

- Explore the connection between the contemporary ecological movement and a lifestyle that dwells in harmony with nature. What social and economic concerns prevent us from viewing the environment as an expression of humanity?
- Interview a practitioner of tai chi about the connection between mind and body.
- Research the influence of Taoism on holistic medical therapies and how Western culture has adopted many Taoist ideas.
- Construct a hypothetical society rooted in the Taoist philosophy. What would a yin leader look like? How would yin values be promoted in education?

"What Does Lao Tzu Mean?"

Taoism employs symbolic language to express the relationship between nature and humanity. Water is a powerful metaphor to explain the misunderstanding that by not using force, we are weak.

Physical Properties	Human Applications
1. It gives way and is yielding.	Do not be arrogant or overambitious.
2. It is infinitely adaptable.	Prepare to deal with whatever situation arises.
3. It tends to low places and it cleanses.	Develop humility.
4. It nourishes all living things by making them better and does not make anything into water itself.	Help improve fellow human beings.
5. It works its way around rigid barriers.	Keep striving to achieve a goal.
6. It is incomparably strong.	There is power among those who can be still and silent.
7. It lies still at the bottom of the ocean despite any storm.	There is peace and quiet deep in our consciousness.
8. It naturally cleans itself when still and finds clarity.	The mind is naturally clear, so foster patience.

Walking Meditation

The simplest way to access reality is to walk. . . .

Walk nowhere, with no purpose except to experience the process of walking, one foot in front of the other. . . .

Look at nothing. Do not become distracted by focusing on anything. Allow your vision to broaden, and you will see everything—all the things you would have missed if your attention had become focused on something. . . .

Listen to nothing. Do not become distracted by the sounds around you, but let them pass through you. As you do, you will hear things you never would have. The same applies to your senses of feeling, taste, and smell and to the emotions that arise from within you. . . .

As you place one foot in front of the other, allow yourself to become aware of the whole method of your walking—the pressure of the ground, the flexing of the muscles, the movement of your skin, the way the weight transfers up your body and down again as you take another step. . . .

Pay attention to your breathing. Count each breath and feel your lungs expand and collapse. Be aware of how each movement is part of your breath and each breath is part of the beat of the universe.

Chapter 8

Shinto

Summaries of the Sources

Through ancient stories and commemorative rituals, the Japanese tradition of Shinto respects the divine character in all beings. It does not oppose other spiritual traditions but instead encourages diverse practices. Practitioners foster humility by embracing the sacred origins of the heavens and earth, where celestial beings still exist in the beauty of mountains, rivers, and other natural formations. Shinto's moral simplicity calls us to worship through action by purifying our minds and bodies.

Excerpt from *Sources of Japanese Tradition:* Shinto Creation Myth

This passage first describes the birth of the Sun Goddess Amaterasu and her responsibility for overseeing the whole creation. The expulsion of Sosa no o no Mikoto represents an evaluation of his moral character and of his disrespect to the elders. By acting in his own self-interest, he does not honor the ancestors and consequently disrespects himself. This episode recognizes the value of a humble disposition toward all created things. Selfishness is not capable of compassionate behavior and therefore is not open to the acceptance of new life.

In deciding to produce children, Amaterasu and Sosa no o no Mikoto honor the lineage that must continue the respect and honor that allowed them to be born of the divine essence. Their decision demonstrates that individual actions always reflect one's familial values and expectations. Furthermore, it is necessary to remember the past of our divine lineage if we are to be successful in the future.

Excerpt from *Motoori Norinaga Zensh:* "The True Tradition of the Sun Goddess," by Motoori Norinaga

The divine transmission of authority is a central focus of this reading. For centuries many secular leaders have claimed a divine right to rule or govern. In this excerpt we find that, according to the Shinto tradition, any recognition of authority must begin with a humble acknowledgment of the creative act of Izanagi and Izanami. Their blessings continue to the present by providing humanity with a human manifestation of the divine—the Japanese emperor. The imperial line directly reflects the descendants of the Sun Goddess.

The Shinto tradition is skeptical of the secular interpretations of these creation myths that represent a divine lineage between the ancient past and the present. Norinaga notes that some people today lack "faith in the wonders of the Divine Age." Contrived explanations and false understandings have been substituted for the awe and wonder of the universe. Though readers may identify an explicit tone of nationalism in Norinaga's writing, reading the selection in the context of Shinto ancestral worship is important. Norinaga emphasizes that because heaven is earth and earth is heaven, there is no need to distinguish between them as if they embody different realms. In praising the natural and political elements in the present, we honor their divine origins. There is no need to create our own traditions or titles, because there is but one true Way.

"The Meaning of *Kami*," by Motoori Norinaga

In this excerpt Norinaga reflects on the concept that is paramount to understanding the Shinto religion—*kami*. Although it may appear trite, *kami* is everything, and everything is in *kami*. It is the pervasive force in the universe that maintains order and harmony. It is not isolated in good people or objects but refers to all objects and beings. It is beyond the dualism of body and spirit. The Western reader can take solace that the incomprehensibility of *kami* is beyond even a scholar such as Norinaga. It represents the ancient time of divine ancestry, in which divine beings' indelible mark was left for us to preserve and cherish.

By identifying various categories of *kami*, Norinaga speaks to the notion that everything shares in the *kami* nature. The placement of *torii* gates in Japan symbolizes the Shinto belief that the sacredness of a place, particularly shrines of worship, is important. Location does not merely designate here or there but also signifies a consciousness of the divine presence of the Goddess and her continued gift of grace. *Kami* is beyond the limits of language and must be experienced aesthetically rather than intellectually.

Activities

Excerpt from *Sources of Japanese Tradition:* Shinto Creation Myth

Guiding the Students Through the Readings

1. Assign the readings as homework. Ask the students, as they read, to reflect on images of the divine in their experiences with world religions. In particular how is gender represented? How does this affect how one prays or identifies with a religious figure such as a saint?

2. Begin the next class period by reminding the students that feminine depictions of the divine are central to many Eastern traditions. The students should notice the emphasis on the attributes and possessions of Amaterasu—her hair, headdress, jewels, and bow and arrows. The correlation between material possessions and celestial stature exemplifies the Shinto recognition that the heavens and earth are one. Moreover Amaterasu's wisdom and justice are traits found also in Western religious traditions. As an example, *Sophia*—the Greek word for "wisdom"—is identified most closely with the goddess Athena. Show images of both Amaterasu and Athena to your students and ask them to note similarities. You will find links to a sampling of images and narratives of Athena and Amaterasu at *www.smp.org.*

3. Return to the readings and draw the students' attention to the creation of the divine imperial ancestors. What do the students think is the reason for listing the deities who were born? Why is the notion of divine lineage or ancestry important to the Shinto way of life?

4. Have the students read the genealogy and infancy narrative in Matthew, chapters 1–2. Compare the two traditions and their understandings of divine lineage. Why are the names and their order important? Are some individuals not included?

5. Summarize the discussion by noting that a religion's genealogy or lineage represents not only its historical longevity but also the authenticity of its tradition.

Excerpts from *Motoori Norinaga Zensh:* "The True Tradition of the Sun Goddess," by Motoori Norinaga / "The Meaning of *Kami*," by Motoori Norinaga

Guiding the Students Through the Readings

1. Before your students read these two selection*s,* ask them to write a reflection on the following questions:

❖ What is your understanding of nature?

❖ Have you ever felt a picture or experience of nature to be religious?

❖ How can the environment be seen to reflect human nature?

2. Assign the readings. Distribute copies of handout 8–A, "What Is *Kami*?" one for each student. Ask the students to complete the handout in class. Have them compare their previous reflections with their handout responses.

3. Have the students choose partners and share their handout answers with each other. When they finish lead a large-group discussion about the relationship between nature and the divine. This will serve as preparation for the next activity.

Going Deeper

This activity examines ecological justice in the world, assessing personal responsibility to respect nature, and constructing an autobiography of our relationship with the earth.

1. Begin by sharing that to cultivate an understanding of *kami*, the students must first evaluate their own connection to the environment. Share the following reflection by Aldo Leopold, an American ecologist:

❖ The land ethic simply enlarges the boundaries of the community to include soils, waters, plants, and animals, or collectively: the land. This

sounds simple: do we not already sing our love for and obligation to the land of the free and the home of the brave? Yes, but just what and whom do we love? Certainly not the soil, which we are sending helter-skelter downriver. Certainly not the waters, which we assume have no function except to turn turbines, float barges, and carry off sewage. Certainly not the plants, of which we exterminate whole communities without batting an eye. Certainly not the animals, of which we have already extirpated many of the largest and most beautiful species. A land ethic of course cannot prevent the alteration, management, and use of these "resources," but it does affirm their right to continued existence, and, at least in spots, their continued existence in a natural state.

(*A Sand County Almanac*, p. 204)

2. Divide the class into groups by having the students count off from one to five. Ask the groups to respond to the following questions:

❖ According to this passage, what is the American land ethic?

❖ How do you see the earth? Is it beautiful, ugly, or somewhere in between?

❖ How do you identify yourself with the natural world? What emotions do you experience when you see a sunset or sunrise? a mountain range? a waterfall?

❖ Is it possible to understand the natural world and the way it works? Explain your answer.

Allow 5 to 10 minutes for group discussions.

3. Have the groups develop three to five moral principles that emerge from their answers to the questions. These can state beliefs about what the relationship should be between humanity and the environment. For example, you might say that recycling contributes to being good stewards of ecology.

Ask the members of the small groups to share with the large group their thoughts on the quotation and questions. Have they ever reflected on the environment this way before? How is it different from considering human ethical situations?

4. Have the students individually reflect on experiences with nature that have influenced their relationship with the earth. Ask what some of the most significant social, cultural, or political developments have been that have affected how they experience the earth.

5. As homework have the students construct a three- to five-page autobiography of their relationship to the earth. Their reflections should draw from the previous questions and group work. Additionally, a section of the paper should develop a concrete proposal to remedy personal or local practices that do not constitute a proper land ethic.

Prayer

Prayer in the Shinto tradition is a ritual performed to coincide with the seasons. These ancient Japanese ritual prayers are called *noritos*. A priest usually recites them. The following is known as the *norito* of the divine garments festival. It pays respect to Amaterasu. It is a simple prayer that expresses the significance of *kami* and its proper worship throughout the year, as follows:

> I humbly speak in the solemn presence
> > Of Ama-terasi-masu-sume-oho-mi-
> > > kami,
> > Whose praises are fulfilled,
> > Where the great shrine posts are firmly
> > planted
> > > And the cross-beams of the roof
> > > soar towards the
> > > > High Heavenly Plain,
> > In the upper reaches of the Isuzu river
> > At Udi in Watarahi:

> I humbly say that the presentation is made
> > Of the woven garments of plain cloth
> > and coarse cloth
> > > Habitually presented
> > > > By the people of the hatori
> > > > and the Womi.
> Thus I humbly speak.

> Say this and present them
> > Also in the Ara-maturi-no-miya. This I
> > speak.
> > > (Donald L. Philippi, *Norito*, p. 59)

After reading the prayer, ask:
- ❖ What do the garments signify in this prayer?
- ❖ What could be the connection between dress and worship?

Action Ideas

- Learn more about the present state of Shinto. How do its beliefs continue to influence modern Japan?
- Explore the relationship between Buddhist practices and Shinto beliefs from Japanese folklore. Study the historical tradition of the *bushido*, or warrior class of the samurai, as an example of this integration of philosophy and action.
- Find examples of when the Shinto tradition has adopted the rituals and practices of other religions. How has it changed these rituals and practices?

What Is *Kami?*

1. Motoori Norinaga begins his meditation on *kami* by noting that "[it] signifies . . . the deities of heaven and earth that appear in the ancient records and also the spirits of the shrines where they are worshipped" (*Motoori Norinaga Zensh*, Tokyo, 1901). In your own religious tradition, where do you see instances of the divine presence in a place of worship? Why are such places necessary?

2. There are instances where rocks, mountains, and other inanimate objects are referred to as *kami*. How is your worldview changed by recognizing that these substances are as valuable as an animal or a human being?

3. Write a description of your understanding of *kami*. Based on the reading, what individuals or locations in nature would you identify as *kami*?

Chapter 9

Judaism

Summaries of the Sources

Honoring God through community and tradition characterizes Jewish life. Abiding by the Commandments in all facets of life is essential. The call as God's Chosen People requires a responsibility to uphold the sacredness of life through rituals and remembrance. Respect for family and elders cultivates the virtue of responsibility, while the search for truth fosters gratitude for learning the faith.

Exodus, Chapters 19–20

This passage from the Book of Exodus describes the liberation of the Israelites from slavery. God conveys his love for his people through the prophetic wisdom of Moses as he teaches the people about their unique Covenant relationship with God. A covenant is a solemn agreement involving mutual commitments between human beings or between God and a human being. The centrality of Moses's prophecy at Mount Sinai is significant because it underscores the importance of the teacher and servant leader in Jewish thought.

The Ten Commandments represent the relational dimension central to the Covenant with the Israelites. By focusing on our relationships with family and acquaintances, we recognize the goodness inherent in all creation. Yet we are also called to remember that the misuse of creation is idolatrous and rejects the gift of life. We are tested, because we struggle to remember the covenant God has placed before us. God should be our sole desire. All accomplishments come from the grace of the gift of creation. Consequently, to worship idols is to place ourselves before our Creator.

Excerpt from *Pirke Aboth: Sayings of the Fathers,* edited with translations and commentaries by Isaac Unterman

Because of the inexhaustible divine nature of God's Word, a plethora of ways exists to interpret its meaning, from the time of the patriarchs to the contemporary age. The Mishnah represents part of the rabbinical collection of such interpretive texts or commentaries on the Torah, which are the first five books of the Hebrew Scriptures. It is important to note that these writings represent a shift from the rich oral tradition that existed during the time of Moses.

This excerpt describes the contributions of Rabbi Hillel to the Jewish commentators. It describes a common question posed to a teacher, one that appears to conflict with the Commandments. In this story it is about holding the Passover sacrifice on the Sabbath, a time when work is forbidden for Jews. Hillel affirms that holding the sacrifice is possible, because he heard a similar answer from his teachers. Hillel's reasoning was sufficient for the local scholars.

Another time he exposed himself to the elements on a rooftop so he could hear two great rabbis of the time. Because of Hillel's respect for the teachers, the elders honored his efforts, which again occurred on the Sabbath. This commitment to education is central to understanding the place of tradition in the Jewish faith. One story explains the virtue of learning through hyperbole—"he knew all the seventy languages of the world, and the language of all the beasts, trees and plants, hills and valleys." We should take the Commandment to love our neighbors as ourselves as a command to serve for the betterment of everyone.

These narratives also direct us to realize that some truths in religious traditions are more important than others. This does not mean particular laws in Judaism are unimportant in kind but rather in degree. A hierarchy of truths exists, in which love of God and neighbor is enhanced by other people. This is what Hillel means when asked to summarize the Torah in one sentence: "What is distasteful unto you, you should not do unto others. This is the entire Torah and the rest is merely an elaboration of this virtue."

Excerpt from *The Family Marko-witz*, by Allegra Goodman

It is common to find a family discussion becoming tense and even hostile. Especially in matters of religious practices, many believers struggle with the tension between the faith of their upbringing and the faith of their young adulthood. Some look for a more liberal approach to their beliefs, while others seek out a more conservative approach. Often the task is to balance the way both faiths speak truth in our lives.

This contemporary novel highlights the tension between tradition and modernity. The elder daughter, Miriam, has embraced a more traditional orthodoxy than has her family. By expounding on how different groups are marginalized or oppressed today, Ed insults his daughter's understanding of the tradition and history explicit in the seder meal. Miriam believes tradition should focus on a literal interpretation of the ritual, whereas her father believes that the story of the Exodus should speak to those afflicted by injustice today.

Respecting the elders is a major tenet of any faith tradition. Honoring our parents, siblings, and extended family is a sign of our renewed commitment to the Abrahamic Covenant and our personal covenant with our loved ones.

Activities

Exodus, Chapters 19–20

Guiding the Students Through the Reading

1. Assign the reading as classwork, asking the students to think about how we can understand the Ten Commandments today. This step could also be assigned as homework.

2. Have the students count off from one to ten. Each number represents one of the Ten Commandments. Place in groups the students who have the same Commandment. If you have fewer than twenty students, assign more than one Commandment to groups as needed. Ask the students to examine their Commandment by answering the following questions:

❖ What is our group's Commandment?

❖ How do people in today's society violate this Commandment?

❖ What obstacles prevent us from fully living in communion with this law?

❖ How can I follow this Commandment more closely?

3. Around the classroom post ten sheets, numbered 1 to 10, from a self-stick easel pad. Each sheet represents one Commandment. Have one student from each group summarize its responses to the questions, writing the summary on the corresponding sheet of posted paper. Survey the writing to ensure the groups have adequately addressed the issues behind the reading.

4. Give each student two self-stick notes and a pen or pencil. Ask the students to write on each note a question or comment about any of the ten groups' responses. When the students finish, invite them to walk around the room and quietly read the various comments and questions. You also may ask for volunteers to serve as curators for each commandment. Ask them to categorize the individual responses any way they choose and to briefly explain how the class has understood the application of the Commandment. For example, they may move the self-stick notes into two columns, where one side contains positive questions or feedback while the other is more critical.

5. Lead a large-group discussion about interpreting historical sources, asking the following questions:

- ❖ What must we consider when reading these documents?

- ❖ Is it possible to interpret these Commandments incorrectly? Why or why not?

- ❖ How can we be faithful to the original context of the Hebrew Scriptures while being creative in applying their teachings to our lives?

- ❖ What are the "idols" of our modern society?

Excerpt from *Pirke Aboth: Sayings of the Fathers,* edited with translations and commentaries by Isaac Unterman / Excerpt from *The Family Markowitz,* by Allegra Goodman

Guiding the Students Through the Readings

1. Assign the readings as homework. Direct the students to write responses to the following:

- ❖ Summarize the readings in your own words.

- ❖ List three examples of how Hillel, Miriam, or Ed recognizes or expresses religious truth.

- ❖ Present an example of how you have struggled to understand something a teacher or family member has said.

2. During the next class period, have the students choose partners and share with each other their responses to the questions. Ask them to note similarities and differences in how they interpreted the questions.

3. For the selection from *Pirke Aboth,* hold a large-group discussion about the characteristics essential for a great teacher. Likewise discuss a student's responsibilities toward the teacher.

4. For the selections from *The Family Markowitz,* have the students discuss where they see themselves as more liberal or conservative than their parents on religious issues. Ask the students whether they identified themselves with any of the characters in particular. Which characters did they identify with and why?

5. Conclude by sharing an account of your own religious development and the effect a teacher or family member had on it. What barriers did you have to overcome to share in the other person's understanding?

Going Deeper

Present the historical and ritual dimensions of Judaism by analyzing various festivals. You may choose festivals or events other than those described on the handout if they apply better to your classroom situation.

1. Distribute copies of handout 9–A, "Jewish Festivals," one for each student. Divide the class into groups of three to four to research the requested information.

2. Discuss the meaning behind rituals and the reflection needed for the rituals to be significant to a religious community. Students may engage in the conversation by considering various commemorative rites in which they actively participate. You may want to explain that tradition is not merely the repetition of an act but also the conscious participation in the memory and transcendent nature of a particular event or person. Symbolic rituals are not just symbols but also call us to ponder the presence of the sacred in the profane.

3. Invite the students to consider how they may continue certain traditions from their families. Encourage the students to talk with family members to learn more about a particular tradition and its meaning. In class ask how students see their faith development as similar to and different from their parents'. What challenges to religious tradition exist today that did not exist or were not as prevalent ten, twenty, or thirty years ago?

4. Summarize with the following points:

❖ Religious truth is not isolated to one event or individual but permeates all who explore and participate in reading history, acting in a ritual, or learning from an elder. Although God's Word is eternal, our understanding of it continues to grow and flourish through myriad questions and answers.

❖ We must be mindful of our religious traditions and work to experience them in our daily lives. By asking "How am I living out this ritual?" we challenge ourselves to model moral behavior for those around us. Our actions should inspire others to act morally too.

Prayer

Many people often use prayer as simply a request for something from the divine. Invite the students to go deeper as they reflect on how their environment—family, friends, and nature—can positively affect their thoughts and actions to know and serve God.

1. Distribute copies of handout 9–B, "Reflections on Prayer," one for each student. Ask five volunteers to read a paragraph each. Allow the large group to pause for silent reflection at the end of each paragraph.

2. Ask the students to write in their journals after listening to the prayer. Have them write about practical ways they can develop deeper prayer lives.

❖ What do you believe is the ultimate purpose of prayer?

❖ Where do you find God's answer to your prayers?

Invite volunteers to share their insights with the rest of the students.

Action Ideas

- Have the students explore where culture and faith intersect and explore the challenges posed to traditional Judaism. In particular explore the different ideas behind Hasidic, Orthodox, and Reform Judaism.
- Have the students learn more about the historical causes of the Holocaust. How have literary figures, along with religious leaders, understood these events?
- Ask the students to research Elie Wiesel and his writings on Jewish culture. What does he mean by the "literature of memory"?
- Invite a local rabbi to speak to your class. Participate in a seder meal to experience the ritual of Passover.

Jewish Festivals

For each festival below, research the historical events that inspired it, the rituals performed—including any objects or artifacts—the time it occurs in the modern calendar, and the possible modern variations or influences on the ritual.

	Purim	Yom Kippur	Sukkoth	Rosh Hashanah	Hanukkah
History					
Rituals performed					
Time of occurrence					
Modern variations or influences					

Reflections on Prayer

by Abraham Joshua Heschel

To pray is to take notice of the wonder, to regain a sense of the mystery that animates all beings, the divine margin in all attainments. Prayer is *our* humble *answer* to the inconceivable surprise of living. It is all we can offer in return for the mystery by which we live. (page 205)

To escape from the mean and penurious, from calculating and scheming, is at times the parching desire of man. . . . Prayer clarifies our hope and intentions. It helps us discover our true aspirations, the pangs we ignore, the longings we forgot. It is an act of self-purification. . . . It teaches us what to aspire to, implants in us the ideals we ought to cherish. (page 206)

Prayer is an invitation to God to intervene in our lives, to let His will prevail in our affairs; it is the opening of a window to Him in our will, an effort to make Him the Lord of our soul. We submit our interests to His concern, and seek to be allied with what is ultimately right. (page 207)

In a sense, prayer begins where expression ends. . . . The soul can only intimate its persistent striving, the riddle of its unhappiness, the strain of living 'twixt hope and fear. Where is the tree that can utter fully the silent passion of the soil? Words can only open the door, and we can only weep on the threshold of our incommunicable thirst after the incomprehensible. (page 208)

The true source of prayer is not an emotion but an insight. It is the insight into the mystery of reality, the *sense of the ineffable*, that enables us to pray. . . . It is in moments of our being faced with the mystery of living and dying, of knowing and not knowing, of love and the inability of love—that we pray, that *we address ourselves to Him who is beyond the mystery*. (page 209)

(The material on this handout is from *The Wisdom of Heschel*, selected by Ruth Marcus Goodhill [New York: Farrar, Straus and Giroux, 1975], pages 205–209. Copyright © 1970, 1972, 1975 by Sylvia Heschel, Executrix of the Estate of Abraham Joshua Heschel.)

Chapter 10

Christianity

Summaries of the Sources

To better explain the Commandment to love our neighbors, these readings reflect the personal faith required to serve in a community of believers. Contemplation and even doubt are elements of the Christian message of hope. To know God we must first discover ourselves, and this knowing often requires a conversion—a change of both mind and heart. Religious experience is essential to realizing that love of self is love of neighbor is love of God.

Matthew, Chapters 5–7

Jesus told parables to express intricate religious concepts through narratives. These stories challenge us to read about how early Christianity developed from being a Jewish sect into the historical faith tradition it is today. When reading this selection, remember Saint Francis of Assisi's call to action: "Preach the Gospel at all times and when necessary use words."

Building on the Old Testament's Decalogue—the first five books of the Bible, which Moses presented—the Sermon on the Mount calls us to conform to God's will and the created order. To live according to the Word of the Father is the path to true joy—not merely worldly happiness, such as gaining prestige or wealth. The corporal and spiritual works of mercy are vital to the lives of Christians, to serve the needs of this world so we may live in glory with the Creator in the next. The Kingdom of God is "already but not yet" built in our lifetimes and calls us to preach the Good News to all we encounter.

The Commandments regarding anger, adultery, divorce, oaths, and retaliation all challenge us to uphold the virtue of charity in all things. Though *charity* is commonly defined in a secular context to mean "almsgiving," here it is better understood as the theological virtue of love that is inherently relational. We should see the Commandments not as negative directives that force us to act in particular ways but rather as positive affirmations of the relationships in our lives. We should cherish all members of the human community and pray even for those who marginalize others. By placing the needs of others before our own, we acquire the grace necessary for our spiritual maturity. We are called to be known by the fruits of our labor, not just for speaking about the injustices in the world.

Excerpt from *Confessions*, by Saint Augustine

This passage from one of the first autobiographies of the Western world demonstrates the introspective nature of Saint Augustine's philosophy. Though his writings have left an indelible mark on the history of Christian theology, his personal experience of God's call is clear from this excerpt.

"Tolle, lege! Tolle, lege!" Augustine heard these Latin words to "take and read" the Scriptures. While reading Romans 13:14–15, he found his call to do away with the concupiscence that ruled his mind and body—the selfish human desire for a person or object. In doing so he modeled the words of the Lord's Prayer, "Thy will be done on earth, as it is in heaven," to submit all thoughts and actions to God. He thus freed himself from the bondage of materialism and was able to see the world with a new heart. Hence comes the idea of conversion—not to change our faith, as

it is commonly misunderstood, but to change our hearts and minds for the better.

Two ideas are central to understanding what Augustine meant by his confession: enjoyment and use. Enjoyment is the attitude toward things we value for themselves. Use is the attitude toward things we value for the sake of something else. In our lives we must learn the right way to enjoy friends and acquaintances just as we should rightly use things for their natural ends, such as the body and its gift of sexuality. Our conscience is not simply what we want but also a vehicle to listen to God's Word in our lives. When we listen as Augustine did, we see the influence of our behavior on those we love most. In Augustine's conversion experience, Saint Monica, his mother, was greatly influential and overcome by joy when he announced his return to God. Although few of us will have such direct contact with God's Word, we should work to hear it in the most unassuming people and places. Conversion is a lifetime commitment to grow in the love of Christ and to bring out that fulfillment in others.

Excerpts from *Concluding Unscientific Postscript to Philosophical Fragments,* by Søren Kierkegaard

This reading presents a complicated philosophical meditation on the nature of faith and the regimented commitment necessary to be called a true Christian. Søren Kierkegaard highlights an individual orientation to faith. He was a pivotal figure in the movement called existentialism, a philosophical school of thought that emphasizes individual experiences to define meaning in a world that is often hopeless. The "what" of doctrine he refers to may be seen as the objective part of Christian faith—rituals, commandments, and history. But knowing the "what" is not sufficient for people to call themselves Christians. For example, the mere fact that a person is baptized does not mean she or he will live like a Christian.

Kierkegaard says we move through three stages of existence. The first is the aesthetic, in which we are concerned with pleasure and enjoyment. The second is the ethical, in which we commit ourselves to act morally. The third and highest is the religious, in which we recognize that suffering is necessary for living. Paradoxically, we become aware of our own objective uncertainty through discovering subjective truth.

We are then confronted with the mystery of faith. On one hand we are called to live lives of service to our neighbors. On the other we are called to sacrifice our lives so we may save them. This requires what Kierkegaard called the "leap of faith," to transcend the rational acceptance of Christianity and to internalize it as part of ourselves. Thus he gives us the dictum "truth is subjectivity." To have a relationship with God, we must first accept the Christian teachings in our lives. We are individuals, yet we flourish in a community of believers. Instead of blindly following the masses (in other writings Kierkegaard notes that "the crowd is untruth"), we must challenge ourselves to live as Christians if we want to be called such. He is not saying that the Christian message itself is subjective but rather that an individual's interpretation of it is. We all face unique and specific circumstances, and therefore the "how" of being a Christian must address those particulars. As a result the truth of the message of Jesus Christ will be confirmed by its universal acceptance. This is what an authentic existence means: to live a faithful life committed to Christian ideals and to call on others to do the same.

Activities

Matthew, Chapters 5–7

Guiding the Students Through the Reading

1. Begin class by having a volunteer read aloud Matthew 7:24–28, in which Jesus says his teaching is a strong foundation for building.

2. Divide the class into three groups. Assign each group to read one chapter from Matthew (chapter 5, 6, or 7). The students may read their assigned chapters either as a group or individually.

3. As the students read, ask them to identify ten teachings that can be seen as foundational to Christianity. For example, in Matthew 5:43–47, followers of Jesus are called to love not only people they like and get along with but also their enemies. (Alternatively, you may assign this step as homework.)

4. Have the students share with the class the foundational teachings they identified. Ask each student to share one unique foundational teaching, continuing until all teachings have been exhausted. Write the teachings on the board as the students mention them.

5. Invite your students to respond to the following questions either in their groups or in a written assignment:

❖ Was it easy or hard to find ten unique foundational teachings in your assigned chapter? Explain.

❖ What are a few common themes in the teachings?

❖ What teachings do you see that are similar to teachings from other faiths we have studied?

❖ What teachings are unique to Christianity?

Excerpt from *Confessions,* by Saint Augustine / Excerpts from *Concluding Unscientific Postscript to Philosophical Fragments,* by Søren Kierkegaard

Guiding the Students Through the Readings

1. Assign the readings from Saint Augustine and Søren Kierkegaard as homework. Distribute copies of handout 10–A, "Faith and Conversion," one for each student. Ask the students to answer the questions as they read.

2. During the next class period, ask the students about reading personal accounts of faith and conversion. Could they identify themselves with any of the ideas or experiences either author wrote about? Explore with the students the benefits and limitations of writing a personal account of faith.

3. Have volunteers share their answers to the handout.

4. Invite the students to write about the stepping stones of their faith journeys. These should include times they encountered someone who influenced them or times they experienced an event that helped make them who they are. Have the students write about how they have lived with their faith traditions, whatever those may be. Ask those students who do not identify themselves with a particular tradition to reflect on why they choose not to call themselves religious or spiritual.

Going Deeper

Faith and doubt are indispensable aspects of living a virtuous Christian life. We are called to believe in things unseen and are confronted with competing messages from contemporary culture. Likewise reason and experience often conflict and create unrest in our hearts when we are asked how we can know and love God. Conduct a large-group discussion exploring how our faith can grow as a result of conflict. Brainstorm solutions to alleviate doubt. Use the following points to begin:

❖ The idea of "privatization" can mean that being religious is a purely individual experience. What are the limits of this explanation? How can a faith community contribute to a personal religious identity? How do other people strengthen our beliefs?

❖ Paul Tillich, an influential Protestant theologian of the twentieth century, once wrote that faith is a matter of ultimate concern. It is an act of the entire person in relation to a God who calls us into relationship. How can our faith in God influence our everyday actions? How do we understand the relationship between ultimate concerns and other concerns such as success or friendship?

Prayer

Distribute copies of handout 10–B, "Prayer Service for the Simplicity of Life and Love," one for each student. The handout provides a prayer by Thomas Merton (1915–1968). Merton was a Trappist monk and writer from the Abbey of Our Lady of Gethsemani, in Kentucky. Ask the students to reflect on a time they felt lost or uncertain about something in their lives. Invite them to consider how their faith has been challenged and how doubt and questions are a normal part of spiritual development. Have the students place themselves in the words of the prayer and to recall specific experiences that may come to them while listening to it. You can read the entire prayer aloud or ask volunteers to read.

Action Ideas

Invite the students to further explore Christianity, its historical precedents, and its growth over two millennia, as follows:

- Research how the cultural phenomenon of postmodernism has interpreted Christian doctrine. Does postmodernism make Christian teachings more accessible or less? Explain.
- Investigate the various denominations of Christianity and how they have responded to the signs of the times.
- Write a chapter from your autobiography about your faith journey. Draw parallels between your life and the conversion experience of Saint Augustine.
- Examine various forms of Christian worship and Churches. Explain how the liturgical rites are universal but differ in their interpretations.
- Document the lives of saints who have experienced a radical transformation. Present your findings to the class. Discuss how God's call is different for everyone.

Faith and Conversion

1. How are Augustine's friend Alypius or his mother, Saint Monica, significant in Augustine's conversion? Based on your reading of the excerpt from *Confessions*, how do you think Augustine understands the nature of friendship? of family?

2. Reflect on the biblical passage that inspired Augustine: "Not in revelling and drunkenness, not in lust and wantonness, not in quarrels and rivalries. Rather, arm yourselves with the Lord Jesus Christ; spend no more thought on nature and nature's appetites." How would you interpret this passage? What challenges prevent you from being "armed with Christ"?

3. How do you see Søren Kierkegaard resolve the paradox of faith?

4. What does Kierkegaard mean when he writes about the lover, "He will hold it fast and appropriate it in a way entirely different from the way he holds anything else, will live in it and die in it, risk everything for it"? Can you explain where this passion is found in your own faith? What would need happen to for someone to experience this kind of emotion?

5. Almost fifteen hundred years separate Saint Augustine and Søren Kierkegaard. Write a fictional dialogue between these Christian philosophers as if they were twenty-first-century contemporaries. Where would they agree? disagree? What would they see as the greatest challenges to the Church today?

(The biblical quotation is from *Confessions,* by Saint Augustine; translated with an introduction by R. S. Pine-Coffin [London: Penguin Books, 1961], page 178. Copyright © 1961 by R. S. Pine-Coffin. Used with permission of Pengin Books, Ltd. The quotation from Søren Kierkegaard is from *Concluding Unscientific Postscript to Philosophical Fragments: Volume 1: Text,* by Søren Kierkegaard; edited and translated by Howard V. Hong and Edna H. Hong [Princeton, NJ: Princeton University Press], page 609. Copyright © 1992 by Princeton University Press.)

Prayer Service for the Simplicity of Life and Love

Justify my soul, O God, but also from Your fountains fill my will with your fire. Shine in my mind, although perhaps this means "be darkness to my experience," but occupy my heart with Your tremendous Life. Let my eyes see nothing in the world but Your glory, and let my hands touch nothing that is not for Your service.

Let my tongue taste no bread that does not strengthen me to praise Your great mercy. I will hear Your voice and I will hear all harmonies You have created, singing Your hymns. Sheep's wool and cotton from the field shall warm me enough that I may live in Your service; I will give the rest to Your poor. Let me use all things for one sole reason: to find my joy in giving You glory.

Therefore keep me, above all things, from sin. Keep me from the death of deadly sin which puts hell in my soul. Keep me from the murder of lust that blinds and poisons my heart. Keep me from the sins that eat a man's flesh with irresistible fire until he is devoured. Keep me from loving money in which is hatred, from avarice and ambition that suffocate my life. Keep me from the dead works of vanity and the thankless labor in which artists destroy themselves for pride and money and reputation, and saints are smothered under the avalanche of their own importunate zeal. Stanch in me the rank wound of covetousness and the hungers that exhaust my nature with their bleeding. Stamp out the serpent envy that stings love with poison and kills all joy.

Untie my hands and deliver my heart from sloth. Set me free from the laziness that goes about disguised as activity when activity is not required of me, and from the cowardice that does what is not demanded, in order to escape sacrifice.

But give me the strength that waits upon You in silence and peace. Give me humility in which alone is rest, and deliver me from praise which is the heaviest of burdens. And possess my whole heart and soul with the simplicity of love. Occupy my whole life with the one thought and the one desire of love, that I may love not for the sake of merit, not for the sake of perfection, not for the sake of virtue, not for the sake of sanctity, but for you alone.

For there is only one thing that can satisfy love and reward it, and that is You alone.

(This prayer is from *New Seeds of Contemplation*, by Thomas Merton [New York: New Directions Publishing Corporation, 1972], pages 44–45. Copyright © 1961 by the Abbey of Gethsemani. Reprinted with permission of New Directions Publishing Corporation.)

Chapter 11

Islam

Summaries of the Sources

Submission is a term used to show how we honor God in all we say and do. Submission is the total surrender of the believer to God. It reminds the believer that all things originate and conclude with God. Islam is rooted in a message of peace and morality, requiring its adherents to abide by daily prayer, almsgiving, and fasting to grow closer to Allah. These are ways in which we offer ourselves in praise and thanksgiving. Muslims learn that by serving others, we will enjoy the glory of the afterlife. Based on this understanding, this chapter's readings reflect the emotional and personal dimensions of practicing one's faith against a secular backdrop.

Excerpt from The Qur'an: Sura 22: The Pilgrimage

The Qur'an represents the oral transmission of God's sacred Word through the Prophet Muhammad. Muslims believe that the archangel of announcements, Gabriel, delivered it and that it embodies the call to offer all blessings and praise to Allah. The magnificence of God is exemplified by the number of titles and designations for him. Islamic beliefs are encapsulated in the Five Pillars, which represent Muslims' core values:

- **Faith.** Believing in the love and mercy of Allah is the requisite step for any Muslim. Faith means acknowledging no other god but Allah and Muhammad as his messenger.
- **Prayer.** Prayer is required five times a day for practicing Muslims. It recognizes the centrality of worship amid the hectic nature of our daily lives.
- **Almsgiving.** Charitable giving is intended to promote the internal growth of individuals while assisting those in most need in society. It is meant to humble the givers by reminding them that all possessions merely reflect God's gift of life.
- **Fasting.** During the month of Ramadan, the ninth month of the Muslim calendar, all Muslims fast from sunrise to sunset and abstain from all physical desires—food, drink, and sexual relations. It concludes with the festival *Eid al-Fitr*. Ramadan reminds us of the need for self-restraint.
- **Pilgrimage.** All Muslims are expected to make the *Hajj*, or pilgrimage to Mecca, at one point in their lives. The *Hajj* follows the path of Muhammad through sacred sites and brings together Muslims from around the world annually. Simple clothes are worn so as not to distinguish class or culture among pilgrims.

This sura in particular emphasizes the role of judgment in God's divine love for humanity.

Properly performing the Five Pillars can aid us in finding favor in the afterlife. To engage in selfish desires and attitudes can only contribute to our separation from the protection of Allah. Behaving in accordance with these customs praises God through the blessings of our lives.

Excerpts from *The Faith and Practice of Al-Ghāzāli,* by W. Montgomery Watt

Many religious traditions have what may be called a mystical dimension, in which individuals discern divine truths through isolation and contemplation. It is primarily experiential, initiated by an intimate and personal encounter with the divine ground of all being. This refers to the nature of Allah, which is recognized both within the practitioner and among other natural phenomena.

In this excerpt from al-Ghazāli, we are introduced to the personal transformation of a devout Muslim who realizes that the search for God must begin with one's own heart. Distracting thoughts and preoccupations with ourselves often encumber our vocations, or callings. By surrendering our egos, we begin the journey to witness the abundance of God's nature, enveloping our every thought, motive, and action. This requires a purification of our senses and bodies so we may listen more closely to the divine message. Finite language cannot capture mysticism. It is ineffable. It represents an ecstatic moment in which we spiritually stand outside ourselves. The culmination is "complete absorption in God." In one respect, our selves return to the divine essence of reality.

Excerpt from "The Tagouris: One Family's Story," by Phyllis McIntosh

The idea of faith is often limited to an internal and private commitment to a particular creed. It is not always something we can recognize in those around us. To witness a person's faith on a personal level, we must be invited into their faith in some way. We should greet this invitation with a sense of respect for the individual. The family in this reading, the Tagouris family, has extended just such an invitation to the reader.

The Tagouris family represents values many in America share: pursuing higher education, taking children to social activities, and meeting the daily demands of professional work. The Tagouris family are also devout Muslims, and their faith greatly impacts their daily life. In this reading the Tagouris family expresses how welcomed they feel by members of their various communities, such as at school and in the workplace. Their

lives consist of a subtle blend of religious expectations and personal choices. For example, the children commute to Islamic classes and receive local tutoring, but Salwa, the mother, recognizes that "you cannot force these things" when asked about her daughters' decision to wear the hijab. For the Tagouris family, faith is an invitation to find God's presence in all areas of life, not simply in a mosque or other sacred space.

This excerpt also demonstrates the power of living by example rather than merely speaking about one's faith tradition. It highlights the concern the Tagouris family has over the use of stereotypes to promote racial or religious intolerance. Their story challenges readers to not base their understanding of Islam on bigotry, misinformation, or biased media portrayals. To recognize the dignity and authenticity of Islamic religious beliefs is to deconstruct the misguided and ignorant representations of our Muslim brothers and sisters (for example, "militant" or "terrorist"). When we enter into dialogue, we come to a fuller understanding of what we hold in common, above what differentiates us.

Activities

Excerpt from The Qur'an: Sura 22: The Pilgrimage

Guiding the Students Through the Reading

1. Assign the reading as homework. Distribute copies of handout 11–A, "Reading the Qur'an," one for each student. The students should write answers to the questions as they read.

2. For the next class period, ask the students to bring in a passage from the Old Testament or New Testament that they feel is similar to the reading from the Qur'an.

3. During the next class period, lead a large-group discussion about the students' impressions of the reading. Remind them that eternal judgment reflects our actions in our lives. In one respect we punish ourselves for not listening to the gift of love God gives us.

4. Invite the students to consider how God could judge them up to now. Ask these questions:

- ❖ Which virtues would you need to develop?

- ❖ Which vices would you need to curtail?

Additionally, ask the students to consider similarities among the monotheistic traditions. These initial reflections will serve as a background discussion to the "Going Deeper" activity later in this chapter.

Excerpts from *The Faith and Practice of Al-Ghāzāli,* by W. Montgomery Watt / "The Tagouris: One Family's Story," by Phyllis McIntosh

Guiding the Students Through the Readings

1. The students should read both selections, noting unfamiliar terms or ideas. Instruct them to compose one question they would ask al-Ghāzāli and one they would ask the Tagouris family about their faith tradition.

2. Have the students choose partners. Let them pose their questions to each other, responding as they think al-Ghāzāli or the Tagouris would respond. Invite them to reflect on what answering as another person is like:

- ❖ For Christian students: Is it difficult to empathize with a Muslim writer?

- ❖ For male students: What challenges you when you speak from a female perspective?

- ❖ For all students: How are both selections similar despite having hundreds of years between them?

3. After the partners have asked their questions of each other, have them find new partners. Ask them to repeat the process of asking and responding to their two questions.

4. Lead a large-group discussion with the following questions:

- ❖ Do you see religion as something personal or public? What examples can you think of for both forms?

- ❖ What danger, if any, would exist if there were no freedom of religious expression?

- ❖ How can we work to learn how cultural practices inform different faith traditions while respecting individuals' privacy?

5. Conclude the discussion by sharing the following with the students:

- ❖ The personal and public expression of one's faith should not be seen as separate identities of our personalities. Rather, they are two sides of the same coin. To bear witness to our religious ideals calls on us to act in solidarity with those who share those principles and with those who disagree. The internal conversion of a person can be an intimate, and perhaps even lonely, experience. This speaks to the unique way God addresses all of us. Religious traditions or symbols need not violate others' sense of privacy, but we must first work to know about others rather than fearing or even rejecting them outright. Our dignity is found in honoring others. Being open to growth means we may have to examine our own beliefs before passing judgment on those around us.

Going Deeper

At this point, students should have a solid grounding in the history and practices of various world religions. You may choose to develop a set of lesson plans that compares two or more of the traditions studied.

1. Distribute copies of handout 11–B, "Comparative Theology," one for each student. Divide the class into three groups. Assign each group to respond to one of the traditions on the handout. Have the students in each group compare their answers with one another. Ask the groups to develop a social action plan to learn more about the concepts and beliefs of monotheism. An example of this may include the following:

- a collection of multimedia images and film that provide an accurate depiction of the monotheistic tradition in question
- a statement to the wider community to advocate for greater dialogue among Jewish, Muslim, and Christian students
- a personal commitment to become an informed citizen of the religious pluralism in the local community

2. Use the students' responses to address misunderstandings or incorrect assumptions. You can also use this handout before a unit as a type of pretest to assess the students' knowledge of the subject matter and to anticipate concepts and ideas that may be unclear.

3. Ask the students to leave their groups and walk around the classroom to speak with at least two other students from different groups about their responses to the handout. Each student should note where others have similar answers or questions, especially a lack of knowledge in the "what do I know?" section of the handout. Ask the students to discuss their uncertainty on particular concepts and also to discuss surprising points of commonality.

4. Summarize the discussion by mentioning that religious understanding is often found on a continuum ranging from absolutism (only one religion has the complete truth) to relativism (all truths are the same). Remind the students that this is not an exercise in superlative religions, where one tradition is somehow qualitatively better than another. The students may struggle with this at first, believing that some beliefs or traditions are foreign and therefore are not correct. You may share that the purpose of doing comparative theology requires that the students first understand the history and beliefs of a particular world religion.

Prayer

The following two prayers are from the thirteenth-century Sufi mystic Jalaleddin Rumi. They capture the spirit of Islamic spirituality through their passion and romantic undertones. One may characterize this tradition as Dionysian, referring to the Greek god Dionysus, the deity of physical and spiritual ecstasy. Poetry like this attempts to describe the indescribable in a religious experience.

1. Invite the students to contemplate the nature of love in their lives. Whom do they love? What do they love? How do they show it? Read the following poem aloud and ask them to close their eyes and listen:

❖ Love comes with a knife, not some
shy question, and not with fears
for its reputation! I say
these things disinterestedly. Accept them
in kind. Love is a madman,

working his wild schemes, tearing off his clothes,
running through the mountains,
drinking poison,
and now quietly choosing annihilation.

A tiny spider tries to wrap an enormous wasp.
Think of the spiderweb woven across the cave
Where Muhammad slept! There are love stories,
and there is obliteration into love.

You've been walking the ocean's edge,
holding up your robes to keep them dry.

You must dive naked under and deeper under,
A thousand times deeper! Love flows down.

The ground submits to the sky and

suffers
what comes. Tell me, is the earth worse
for giving in like that?

Don't put blankets over the drum!
Open completely. Let your spirit-ear
listen to the green dome's passionate
murmur.

Let the cords of your robe be untied.
Shiver in this new love beyond all
above and below. The sun rises, but
which way
does night go? I have no more words.

Let souls speak with the silent
articulation of a face.

(Coleman Barks, *Rumi: The Book of
Love*, pp. 47–48)

2. Invite the students to react to the poem. What words or images stood out for them? Were they reminded of something? Did they feel anything?

3. Conclude by reading this second prayer by Rumi. You may want to refer to the place of dancing in Sufi mysticism. The whirling dervishes practice a ritual dance known as *sema*, a form of ecstatic prayer and meditation:

Dance, when you're broken open.
Dance, if you've torn the bandage off.
Dance in the middle of the fighting.
Dance in your blood.
Dance, when you're perfectly free.

(P. 138)

4. Ask the students to compose their own poetry to express their feelings about love or a significant relationship in their lives. Instruct them not to follow any particular rhyme scheme. Remind them that authentic prayer should be an emotional response to God's love. These poems are very personal, and you may not wish to take any more action. Or remembering the poems' personal nature, you may want to invite the students to share their poems or simply to turn them in to you.

Action Ideas

- Further explore the mystical tradition of Sufism through its poetry and rituals.
- Introduce the students to Islamic instrumental songs that may be used as background music for meditation.
- Research the suras from the Qur'an that discuss the concept of *jihad*. How have the mainstream media misconstrued this idea? What may be done to undo the ethnic stereotyping that occurs when ignorance hinders us from recognizing Islam as a peaceful religion?
- Visit a local mosque and write a report on your experience. Try to interview an imam (the spiritual head of a Muslim community) during your visit. Describe how the central beliefs of Islam are expressed visually. In particular, why will you not find a painting or other depiction of the Prophet Muhammad?
- Learn more about the theological beliefs and practices of the Sunni and Shia branches of Islam and how their beliefs reflect their understandings of the message of Muhammad.

Reading the Qur'an

Answer the following questions based on your reading of the Qur'an:

1. What is a pilgrimage? How can participating in one be seen as a form of prayer or worship?

2. What will happen on the Day of Judgment? How will people be rewarded or punished?

3. Where do you see reference to the Five Pillars? Is one pillar emphasized in particular?

4. What challenges await Muhammad as he assumes the role of prophet?

5. Interpret the meaning of the following quotation, paying close attention to which Commandment it represents: "People, here is an illustration, so listen carefully: those you call on beside God could not, even if they combined all their forces, create a fly, and if a fly took something away from them, they would not be able to retrieve it. How feeble are the petitioners and how feeble are those they petition!"

(The quotation on this handout is from *The Qur'an,* a new translation by M. A. S. Abdel Haleem [New York: Oxford University Press, 2004], page 214. Copyright © 2004, 2005 by M. A. S. Abdel Haleem.)

Comparative Theology

Fill out the following chart based on your understandings and experiences of the monotheistic traditions listed and their understanding of the following concepts and figures: (1) the nature of God, (2) the person of Jesus Christ, (3) the role of prophets, (4) the afterlife and judgment, and (5) the forms of prayer.

	Nature of God	Person of Jesus	Role of Prophets	Afterlife and Judgment	Forms of Prayer
Christian view (what I know)					
Christian view (what I want to know)					
Jewish view (what I know)					
Jewish view (what I want to know)					
Muslim view (what I know)					
Muslim view (what I want to know)					

Chapter 12

A World of Perspectives

Summaries of the Sources

The previous chapters have not addressed an abundance of other faith traditions in our society. This chapter addresses many of them. This chapter's selections reflect the pluralism of religious thought in America today. By reflecting the diversity of the world, this chapter may also be understood as a preface to postmodern religion. *Postmodernism* in this context refers to the limits of language and normative concepts to comprehend the depth of religious experience. We find a range of sacred experiences that may be entirely "other" to our own in representing values and practices we have not either experienced or learned about. Various paths to truth are described: asceticism, universalism, revelation, millennialism, secularism, psychology, and ecology. These selections help us understand that diversity itself is a feature of the divine.

Jainism: Excerpt from the *Acáránga Sutra*

Jainism can reflect a spiritual ideal that focuses on a strictly ascetic standard of living. Fasting not only brings about a sense of humility and empathy with those who suffer but also requires the mental clarity to be mindful of the task at hand. In this passage we see that the final fast for the monk is grounded in a penitent act to make amends for the indulgences of the body. Joy is found in the ability to overcome mental obstacles and participate in our own salvation. Religion therefore is the complete surrender of our physical state of being so we may ourselves be transformed and transform others. This underscores the doctrine of nonviolent resistance, because when we engage in violence, we presume that the body is of the utmost significance. Jainism teaches quite the opposite: our bodies serve as the medium through which we become enlightened.

Baha'i: Excerpt from the *Kitab-i-Aqdas*

The Baha'i tradition is characterized by its universality. It recognizes and respects the prophets of world religions as authentic messengers of the divine word. This passage emphasizes the two seminal obligations: the recognition of God as the origin of all creation and the moral duty that must be shown to all humans in the spirit of serving God. It employs the metaphor of sleep to teach that many people are unaware of these obligations and continually serve themselves by desiring false idols. The knowledge God possesses is available to those who are able to dismiss the temptations of the world.

The reading from *Kitab-i-Aqdas* concludes with a meditation on what we can truly call ours. Material objects may give the illusion that we can own them, but that is a limited perspective. We need to become regimented in learning about the only thing that is eternal and secure—God. We do not profit by accumulating wealth and possessions in this world but rather flourish when our existence is offered in thanksgiving to the Almighty. After death we are all accounted for in the same way. If everyone knew this from the outset, they would renounce their possessions and seek refuge in the calling to eternal life.

Mormonism: Excerpt from "Joseph Smith—History: Extracts from *The History of Joseph Smith, the Prophet*"

Mormonism embodies the revelation of God to the prophet Joseph Smith. These accounts were recorded into what is now known as the Book of Mormon; this revelation follows the New Testament. This selection recalls the persecution Joseph Smith experienced from informing people he had a vision. This is a difficult notion for many to understand, because visions are by nature personal phenomena of religious intimacy. In this account we find the angel Moroni revealing where he buried the golden plates that contain the writings of the early Christian Church. They represent the fulfillment of the revelations Jesus Christ made and signify the unity of people of all languages and traditions. The witness of Smith explains the awe and reverence that comes from listening to the Word of God. Revelation is foundational to understanding how this message is beyond culture and historical place. However, not everyone is called to serve as a prophet and challenge others to repent by coming to know God in their lives.

Jehovah's Witnesses: Excerpt from *Awake!:* "Where Is This World Headed?"

Jehovah's Witnesses, as reflected by their very name, seek to bring the Word of God to all peoples. They believe that the decline of values and community are signs that the end of time is approaching. Preparation is essential to receive these teachings and to repent of our selfish desires and behaviors. Biblical literalism is a feature of the Jehovah's Witnesses, who believe that the Word of God is not meant for interpretation or correction, but rather that the writers of the Christian canon were simply conduits of the divine Word.

In this reading we find a reflection on the phrase *the last days.* Theologically, this refers to what is known as millennialism, whereby the Bible serves as a template for how we are to be saved. The first step is to repent of our sins. In this millennial tradition, it is pivotal to calculate the time when this final judgment will take place. Jesus's teachings are all that is needed to save the faithful. By reading the cultural signs of war and conflict, we are able to read what the Bible has foretold.

Secular Humanism: Excerpt from *The Gay Science:* "Parable of the Madman," by Friedrich Nietzsche

Secular humanism focuses on the role of reason over faith and seeks to clarify moral principles without supernatural explanations. The exemplar of this position is Friedrich Nietzsche, whose writings in the nineteenth century served as the foundation for the "death of God" philosophical movement. The phrase is not meant literally but refers to the end of humanity's need to believe in an omniscient creator. What is real is what Nietzsche calls the "will to power," the means by which an individual forges meaning from an otherwise futile existence. Rather than the morality of the masses, which comes from the Judeo-Christian worldview, Nietzsche upholds the person as the center of value and meaning. Because reason is suspect, we must find solace in our subjectivity where we construct reality. Nietzsche posits the *Übermensch,* "the Overman," who is able to affirm his own existence creatively without needing a faith or institution to do it for him.

The "Parable of the Madman" reminds us of the story about the Greek philosopher Diogenes, who walked throughout Athens with a lamp in daylight looking for an honest man. Nietzsche's parable draws attention to the inability of everyday people to realize they live *as if* God were dead. The image of a madman demonstrates that it is not the search for truth that drives humanity mad but rather the possession of it. The madman knows God is dead, but those around him are unable or unwilling to accept this truth. Nietzsche's use of persistent questioning can be read as a critique of dogmatic affirmations presented by institutional religions. He concludes by noting how genuine awareness takes time, as we make meaning retrospectively.

Scientology: Excerpt from *Dianetics: The Modern Science of Mental Health,* by L. Ron Hubbard

Scientology can be misunderstood when its teachings are interpreted through popular media outlets. The teachings of L. Ron Hubbard focus on what may be characterized as a Gnostic perspective of religion, in which certain individuals are endowed with the clarity to perceive reality. This chapter's passage refers to the process of becoming a clear—to be without false mental dispositions. Dianetic therapy refers to a form of psychoanalysis, a therapeutic rehabilitation that asks patients to reflect on their unconscious behaviors. This form of analysis contends that our state of mind is the manifestation of its social environment. Consequently neuroses and ills can be alleviated through introspective questioning. This is supplemented by heightening the physical senses. Yet these same senses are capable of creating a false personality for a person who has not become a clear. To face reality Scientology teaches that we must first face ourselves.

The Old Religion of the Goddess: Excerpt from *Dreaming the Dark: Magic, Sex and Politics,* by Starhawk

Starhawk begins this reading by recalling the various names and origins of the "Old Religion." The Old Religion embraces its Judeo-Christian roots and indigenous myths, all the while adapting itself to the dynamic movement of the Spirit. Its rich symbolism reflects the divine presence in nature.

What differentiates the Old Religion of the Goddess from the other religions examined in this chapter is its emphasis on the immanent nature of religion. It has no need for a transcendent form of divinity, because our connection to nature is our primary relationship. The Goddess embodies the feminine qualities that illustrate our relationship with nature. This is known as an "ecofeminist" viewpoint. The experience of ritual is intended to change our consciousness and to reinforce the sacred bond among the communities of the natural world. The historical origins of the Old Religion of the Goddess recognize that power is first and foremost a creative and nurturing influence. Moreover, this strength values the sexual dimension inherent in human nature.

Starhawk also refers to the patriarchal influence that prioritized class and prestige over ecology. Rather than promoting a both / and approach, in which both feminine and masculine features of the world are honored, the modern period advocated an either / or position, which created an aura of suspicion toward pagan practices. As with other persecuted religions, followers of the Old Religion of the Goddess were forced to worship in secret as they gathered in covens to protect the sanctity of their rituals. Our contemporary era is marked by a culture that promotes egoism and the advancement of the individual. The Old Religion challenges us to recall our first relationship with Mother Earth and to see it as the paradigm for all our relationships.

Activities

Mormonism: Excerpt from "Joseph Smith—History: Extracts from *The History of Joseph Smith, the Prophet*"

Guiding the Students Through the Reading

1. Assign the reading as homework. Ask the students to answer the following three questions as they read:

- ❖ How do you understand the nature of revelation?

- ❖ What are the role and purpose of a modern-day prophet?

- ❖ What differences and similarities are you aware of between Mormonism and other Christian denominations?

2. During the next class period, invite the students to choose partners and share their reactions to the reading and questions. You may want to share with them the modern difficulty of recognizing truth in spiritual revelations. We often ask for empirical proof of religious truths, although they do not lend themselves to that type of inquiry.

3. In the large group, ask the students to share their reactions to the reading and discussion. Distribute copies of handout 12–A, "Mormonism," one for each student. Have the students read it quietly before raising questions or making comments.

4. Hold a large-group discussion examining the beliefs of the Church of Jesus Christ of Latter-day Saints. What influence have the media or contemporary culture had on the students' understanding of Mormonism?

Baha'i: Excerpt from the *Kitab-i-Aqdas* / Jehovah's Witnesses: Excerpt from *Awake!:* "Where Is This World Headed?" / Secular Humanism: Excerpt from *The Gay Science:* "Parable of the Madman," by Friedrich Nietzsche / The Old Religion of the Goddess: Excerpt from *Dreaming the Dark: Magic, Sex and Politics,* by Starhawk

Guiding the Students Through the Readings

1. Assign the readings as homework. Ask half the students to read the selections from Baha'i and the Jehovah's Witnesses. Have the other students read the selections from secular humanism and the Old Religion of the Goddess. As additional homework ask the students to develop one question about the faith traditions and two understandings of the traditions based on each reading they are assigned.

2. During the next class period, in the large group, have the students summarize the understandings and pose the questions they created. From what all the students share, ask them to choose two questions and four understandings for each reading. Inform them that these will be used to help the other students.

3. Have the students exchange with those who did the other readings the questions and reflections they created. For example, a student who read the selections from secular humanism and the Old Religion of the Goddess should exchange questions and understandings with a student who did not read them.

4. Assign the students to read the other two selections they have not already read.

They should respond to the questions they received in step 3. They should use the understandings to guide their comprehension. Ask the students to reflect on the experience of using questions their peers created. Would they add other insights to the understandings given to them? Did they know answers to the questions?

5. Summarize the lesson by asking the students to comment on the following:

❖ How do these four readings think about what it means to be "religious"?

❖ What similarities did the pairs of readings have?

Share with the students that these four readings may be categorized by these distinctions—nature vs. revelation, secular vs. religious, and immanent vs. transcendent. The selections from secular humanism and the Old Religion of the Goddess represent the categories of nature, secular, and immanent. On the other hand, the selections from Baha'i and the Jehovah's Witnesses represent the categories of revelation, religious, and transcendent. Each pairing represents the duality prevalent in theological discourse.

Going Deeper

The following activity provides an opportunity for the students to learn about postmodernism as an approach to include divergent perspectives on religious practices. Though this allows several religious minorities to be heard, it can also promote the relativity of truth and a suspicion of authority and social structures. Use this background to explore where your students locate truth and how it pertains to their faith formation.

1. Divide the class into four groups and ask them to brainstorm their understandings of culture—the shared values, practices, and norms of a society. As "culture" we may also consider the influence of popular culture and media outlets that contribute to our understanding of relationships in both secular and religious contexts. How is this notion of culture defined? Who or what defines it? Has it changed or remained the same? What role has the students' faith played in addressing these questions?

2. After the students have a few minutes to discuss these questions in their groups, ask them individually to write down responses to the following questions:

❖ What aspect of American culture has influenced you the most?

❖ What aspect of American culture do you feel you have contributed the most to or have helped to create?

The students may be reluctant at first to openly discuss their affinity for cultural values or beliefs, but it is important that you begin where they are in their journeys to find truth. Have the students share this written reflection with their group members.

3. Distribute copies of handout 12–B, "Postmodern Faith Formation," one for each student. Ask the students to read the article to themselves. Then assign to each group one of the four considerations from the article—authority, diversity, relevance, and justice. For their assigned consideration, the students should answer the following question and provide an explanation:

❖ Do you agree or disagree with the premise of the writer's thesis that there is a strong need for the "new" Church to address the concerns of adolescents while inviting them to find truth in a faith community?

4. Ask each group to explore its members' personal understandings of the article. Do any of the readings from this chapter address the ideas in Muldoon's article?

5. Conclude the discussion by saying something along these lines:

❖ Catholicism, by definition, recognizes the universal search for truth. However, numerous social expressions have attempted to define truth by denying the existence of God, withdrawing trust from religious leaders, or finding solace in their naïveté about the truths of world religions. The formation of adolescent spirituality is essential to the life of the Church and its members. Though the search for truth must find a place in our individual culture and language, it calls us to rediscover the fellowship known by all humanity. Growth in our knowledge of the Catholic tradition should not require us to abandon the search for creative ways to value authority, embrace diversity, stipulate relevance, and seek justice for all. These may be considered to be the four postmodern marks of the Church.

Prayer

This prayer activity is a reflection on some principles to consider when engaging in discussions about other religious traditions. Their original formulation was by the Rev. Krister Stendahl, who served as dean of Harvard Divinity School and was the Lutheran bishop of Stockholm, Sweden. During his tenure in Stockholm, the Church of Jesus Christ of Latter-day Saints built a temple, which caused controversy among the locals. Bishop Stendahl affirmed the need to be open to pluralism and raised his three principles at a press conference in 1985. Since then, there have been various iterations of these guidelines for dialogue.

Distribute copies of handout 12–C, "Prayer Service: Prayer for Diversity," one for each student. This prayer service presents these principles and invites the students to reflect on them. Lead your students in the prayer by reading each principle aloud, followed by the reflection question, allowing time for the students to reflect silently on each principle and question.

Action Ideas

- Research the teaching and practices of one of the traditions summarized in this chapter. What makes it a religion?
- Write a report on a religious institution not discussed in this chapter. Why do you feel it would merit inclusion? What reservations would you have about including it?
- Summarize the origins of different contemporary faith traditions. Are they based on personal revelations? Do they share points of commonality with the selections discussed in this chapter?
- Explore the relationship between secular humanism and theology.

Mormonism

Following is a summary of the central teachings of the Church of Jesus Christ of Latter-day Saints (LDS), also known as Mormons, named after the prophet Mormon—the father of the angel Moroni, who appeared to Joseph Smith. Moroni assembled the records of the first inhabitants of North America. This summary serves as a brief introduction to Mormonism's religious beliefs.

Jesus Christ

The person of Jesus Christ is revered as the only Son of God. He lived a perfect life on earth and served as a moral paradigm for others. He atoned for our sins through his agony in the garden at Gethsemane and his Crucifixion. The principles of this Gospel message entail faith in the person of Christ, repentance, Baptism, and the laying on of hands to receive the Holy Spirit. Baptism—required to be a member of the LDS and eventually to enter the Reign of God—does not occur until age eight, which is believed to be the age of accountability. Continuing faithfully to follow Jesus's message is known as enduring to the end, through personal responsibility and fidelity to his Commandments.

Revelation

Jesus Christ established his Church through the Twelve Apostles, and he also appointed the priesthood, comprising missionaries, patriarchs, presiding leaders, and elders. Mormons believe the president of the LDS to be a living prophet and the rightful successor to Joseph Smith. The presidents trace their authority through the Apostles to Jesus Christ in an uninterrupted chain of ordinations. Only males can serve in this role. As part of the restoration of the Gospel, God revealed truth in four books of scripture that Mormons use. These are the Doctrine and Covenants (teachings on matters such as the eternal nature of families and dietary regulations), the Book of Mormon (the record of God's communication with the people who lived in the ancient Americas), the Pearl of Great Price (earlier writings of Joseph Smith, with translations of the writings of Abraham), and the Christian Bible.

Community

The Mormon community requires its members to practice charitable giving by enforcing tithing, the biblical mandate to donate one-tenth of one's income, to help build up the Church. Tithing also serves the community when a member faces financial difficulties. Debt is to be avoided at all costs. Additionally, missionaries serve in an essential capacity to spread the Gospel of Jesus. With thousands of men and women serving around the world for up to two years, typically beginning after high school, Mormons believe they are fulfilling their covenant with God to witness to the love of Christ. The centrality of the family is paramount for LDS faith and is seen in the modesty of the thoughts and behaviors of Mormons.

Judgment

Through the atonement of Jesus, it is believed we will be resurrected and saved from a physical death. Original Sin was the responsibility of Adam and Eve, and we will not be punished for their transgression. All people, regardless of their being moral or evil, will receive immortality through the power of Christ. However, only those who have followed the Gospel Commandments will receive eternal life, the highest state we can achieve. One of three kingdoms awaits us in the afterlife, depending on the life we have lived—the celestial (the highest, where Jesus and God reign), the terrestrial (for those who have not accepted the laws of God but have lived moral lives), and the telestial (for those who remain sinful and need to repent). Ultimately, individuals are responsible for working out their own salvation through prayer, reading of the Scriptures, and living chaste lives according to the laws and ordinances of God.

Postmodern Faith Formation

by Timothy P. Muldoon

Many pre–Vatican II U.S. Catholics were raised in a Catholic culture that nurtured their faith. Many parishes followed ethnic lines in cities, had parochial schools, and provided the primary forum for socialization in American culture. Today, in contrast, inner-city parishes are struggling as Catholics have moved into a suburban, mobile, dispersed culture in which parish life is but one more activity to fit into an already busy schedule. Young people in many cases have not been raised with the same commitment to Catholicism that their parents or grandparents developed and thus do not share the same roots in the Church. . . .

The mistake that many educators make in teaching young people about Christianity is to assume that *telling* someone a truth is the same as the other person *believing* it as truth. An important factor that affects evangelization and formation today is a skeptical attitude toward authority—a factor that was almost absent from my grandparents' generation. Today, people have a more sophisticated attitude toward authority, especially since a person can so easily confront different claims to authority with the click of a mouse or the changing of a channel. Many young adults look upon religious questions in a pragmatic way: It is true if it affects me directly.

Unfortunately, many young adults have seen no practical need to appropriate Catholic faith, and so they approach religious questions with what seems to many to be an appalling naiveté. Under these circumstances, it can be difficult to address the topic of faith formation. To put it frankly, religious educators can take nothing for granted—they must assume (at least initially) that young adults have no substantive knowledge of the Catholic tradition. Eventually, of course, it will become evident that many young adults have developed a more sophisticated understanding of faith; but for the sake of formation, it is still important to make no premature conclusions. This may appear to some as patronizing, but I suggest that it creates a relationship between the educator and the young adult in which faith formation will be an unfolding dialogue rather than a lecture. If faith is an invitation, then faith formation will be a process of discovery. Faith formation will simply not work for a large number of young people if it is perceived as yet another body of information that must be learned. The bottom line is that those who respond, even with reservation, to the invitation of Jesus will seek for themselves answers to the questions they raise and will seek out people who can help them. . . .

Four Considerations for Inculturating Catholic Faith Among Young Adults

I shall focus on four: authority, diversity, relevance, and justice. I shall suggest that faith formation for young adults must be regarded not merely as an activity of a parish office, but rather, a process that must integrate the entire parish in all its aspects: liturgy, preaching, programming, evangelization, socialization, and the whole of parish life. Ultimately, the emphasis on faith formation is the practice of growing as a church, like the response of the apostles to the experience of Pentecost.

Authority
Young people's attitude toward authority has been shaped to a great extent by the culture. That many are suspicious of authority is not surprising; this attitude seems to be a part of maturing.

What is new, however, is the sheer volume of claims to authority that young people confront on a regular basis. . . .

Diversity

A second important consideration among young adults is diversity. Unlike many older Catholics, young adults are likely to know many people of different racial, ethnic, and religious backgrounds, and are thus less likely to see Catholicism as the one "true" church. In response to this attitude, I usually refer to Catholicism as a "wisdom tradition," a term that may also be applied to other faiths. Rather than watering down the meaning of Catholic faith, this term is meant to connote something of what we find in the *Declaration on Religious Liberty (Dignitatis Humanae)* of the Second Vatican Council: namely, that the different faiths of the world are rich sources of human understanding, and that we can learn from them all even while holding that the fullness of truth subsists in the Catholic Church. . . .

Relevance

By now it should be clear that the concern for relevance is a pervasive one. Young adults need to know how Catholic faith speaks to their questions, their desires. Because we live amidst a marketplace of ideas, evangelization takes on an economic flavor: we must "sell" the truth by showing what it means to the "spiritual consumer." . . . It is of fundamental importance to show that the Catholic tradition of wisdom is not merely an abstract notion, but rather, one that enables people to live the good life. For this reason, the relevance concern is closely tied to the final concern of justice.

Justice

Young people today, like those of the previous generation, recognize that concern for the welfare of the person and of society extends to the poor, the sick, the disenfranchised, the outcast. Unlike so many bland egocentric claims to authority in the religious marketplace, Catholic tradition emphasizes solidarity with the poor, and this emphasis can help young people understand how Catholicism is more than just another set of rules. . . .

Conclusion

Rather than lamenting the sorry state of faith formation among young adults, we can take comfort in the fact that young adults still show a great deal of interest in religious questions. Traditional thinking suggests that the future of the Church depends on people having a strong sense of belonging to the Church, knowledge of its traditions and liturgy, and a commitment to its future. I suggest, however, that even though young adults as a group may be less knowledgeable about their faith than their counterparts of a generation ago, this need not be a cause for despair. Indeed, if we take seriously the far-reaching impact of Vatican II, we cannot be too surprised. The Church changed dramatically one generation ago, which means that we who grew up in this "new" Church are only now coming into our adult years. It is reasonable to expect, then, that our cohort must formulate a language of faith different in some ways from that of the previous generation. What I have sought to show are some ways in which educators can appropriate the concerns of young adults, in order to help them to draw from the wisdom of the Catholic tradition. The gospel notion of the wedding banquet is illustrative here: many young people are like those who have either not understood or not received the invitation of the Father; thus he sends his stewards out to find them, that they might not find themselves starving outside the banquet hall.

(The material on this handout is from "Starving Outside the Banquet Hall: Young Adults and Their [Hunger for] Faith Formation," by Timothy P. Muldoon, in *The Living Light*, Fall 2000, volume 37, at *www.usccb.org/education/catechetics/livlghtfall2000.shtml#muldoon*, accessed October 13, 2008. Copyright © 2000 by the United States Conference of Catholic Bishops, Washington, D.C. Used with permission. All rights reserved.)

Prayer Service: Prayer for Diversity

1. If you want to know what others believe, ask them. We should not bear false witness to religions by assuming we know their teachings. People should read primary sources and hear from believers directly. **Reflection:** Have there been times when I have assumed something about another person?

2. When comparing teachings, compare your ideal to their ideal. Do not compare your ideal to their worst. For example, do not compare the lives of Catholic saints to Islamic terrorists when discussing the doctrine of salvation. Any comparison should be based on the center of the religious spectrum so as not to believe that radical religious ideologies are the norm. **Reflection:** How can I learn to challenge cultural and religious stereotypes?

3. You should leave room for "holy envy." This is when you discover something in another religion that inspires you but that is not your own. You do not attempt to make it part of your tradition but revere its uniqueness and place in the religion of others. This allows us to mature in our own faith while appreciating the diversity of religious practices that exists in the world. **Reflection:** What beliefs or practices have I grown envious of in my studies?

4. We should trust in the Golden Rule. Indian and Chinese sages articulated loving-kindness centuries before the time of Christianity. The Golden Rule of treating others as we would like to be treated is a "catholic" teaching insofar as it is universal. The emphasis on morality is paramount to every religious tradition. **Reflection:** How do I model behavior that genuinely respects others and considers their differences?

5. Diversity itself is evidence for the need to cultivate an aesthetic and cultural appreciation for diverse religions. Cultural pluralism is the hallmark of human existence, and we should consider the words of Max Müller (1823–1900): "The person who knows about one religion, understands none." Learning about world religions is necessary for living and thriving in a global community. **Reflection:** How do I mature as an individual when I learn more about my global community?

Closing Prayer

Loving God,

You are known by many names but remain the same source of hope and joy for all your children.

Bless me with eyes to see with compassion all of your children.

Bless me with a voice to ask serious and respectful questions of those from whom I have differing views.

Bless me with ears to hear all your children without prejudice or discrimination.

Bless me with hands to reach out and share your mercy and love.

Bless me with a heart that always seeks you in all your wondrous creations.

Appendix

Additional Resources

The following are additional resources corresponding to each chapter. Included in this annotated list are books, articles, and audiovisual resources. See *www.smp.org* for links to Web sites related to the chapter topics.

Chapter 1: The Catholic Church and World Religions

Dupuis, Jacques, SJ. *Toward a Christian Theology of Religious Pluralism*. Maryknoll, NY: Orbis, 1999.

> In this systematic treatment of world religions, the Belgian Jesuit Jacques Dupuis examines the issue of salvation and how the love of God can be mediated through other traditions. He advocates for an inclusive theology that embraces differences.

Hefling, Charles, and Stephen J. Pope, eds. *Sic et Non: Encountering Dominus Iesus*. Maryknoll, NY: Orbis, 2002.

> This collection of essays studies the 2000 document *Sic et Non,* by the Congregation for the Doctrine of the Faith. The document affirms the centrality of Jesus Christ for human salvation. It offers a critical and thorough look at the Catholic position on non-Christian religions.

Pontifical Council for Inter-Religious Dialogue. *Dialogue and Proclamation: Reflection and Orientations on Interreligious Dialogue and the Proclamations of the Gospel of Jesus Christ*. 1991. Found at *www.vatican.va/roman_curia/ pontifical_councils/interelg/documents/ rc_pc_interelg_doc_19051991_dialogue-and-proclamatio_en.html.*

> This reflection on the twenty-fifth anniversary of *Nostra Aetate* examines the steps necessary to engage in a Christian appraisal of other religious traditions. It presents the benefits of and obstacles to dialogue and the role of the universal Church in a world of pluralism.

Chapter 2: Primal Religious Traditions

Neihardt, John G. *Black Elk Speaks*. Lincoln, NE: Bison Books, 2004.

> This classic biography of the great Lakota leader Nicholas Black Elk details the journey to unite humanity and nature against the backdrop of triumph and tragedy in nineteenth-century America.

Sitting Bull: Chief of the Lakota Nation. A&E Video, 2005 (60 minutes, not rated).

> Sitting Bull was one of the last great leaders of Indian resistance. He helped defeat Gen. George Custer's army at the Battle of the Little Big Horn, in Montana. This biography looks at the Lakota medicine man through his early fights with settlers and his leadership to overcome adversity.

Chapter 3: Hinduism

Hemenway, Priya. *Hindu Gods: The Spirit of the Divine*. San Francisco: Chronicle Books, 2003.

> This illustrated book provides profiles of the major gods and goddesses in Hinduism. It provides a succinct description of this complex tradition while showing the divine imagination of its visual arts.

Monsoon Wedding. Universal Studios, 2001 (115 minutes, rated R).

> This complex film describes the social and religious tensions behind a traditional Hindu Punjabi wedding. This movie is rated R, so show only preselected scenes. For the viewers who are minors, obtain parental permission to view an R-rated movie, and use your best judgment about the appropriateness of the film and the advisability of viewing relevant excerpts.

Puja: Expressions of Hindu Devotion. Smithsonian Institution, 1998 (29 minutes, not rated).

> This video presents a brief overview of the local customs surrounding the *puja* ritual. It explains the ritual's significance and place in Hindu spirituality.

Water. Twentieth Century Fox, 2006 (117 minutes, rated PG).

> The film examines the plight of a group of widows forced into poverty. It focuses on a relationship between one of the women, who wants to escape the social restrictions imposed on widows, and a man who is from the highest caste and a follower of Mohandas Gandhi.

Chapter 4: Buddhism

Dalai Lama, The: The Four Noble Truths. Mystic Fire Video, 2002 (360 minutes, not rated).

> In this video, the Dalai Lama reflects extensively on the nature of the Four Noble Truths of Buddhism. He reinforces the belief that we must empty ourselves of desire before we can attain enlightened self-awareness.

Fisher, Robert E. *Art of Tibet*. New York: Thames and Hudson, 1997.

> This collections of Tibetan paintings and sculptures explores the Tibetan school of Buddhist thought through its various symbols, rituals, and iconography.

Suzuki, Shunryu. *Zen Mind, Beginner's Mind*. Boston: Shambhala, 2006.

> This introductory text is from one of the great Zen masters, who teaches that the power of meditation allows the individual to find enlightenment and tranquility.

Thich Nhat Hanh's Mindful Movements: Gentle Contemplative Exercises with the Monks and Nuns of Plum Village. Sounds True Video, 1998 (38 minutes, not rated).

> This introduction to mindful meditation is led by Zen master Thich Nhat Hanh, who guides viewers through a series of gentle exercises created specifically to cultivate a joyful awareness of the body and breath. These are the same meditations in motion that the monks and nuns of Plum Village Monastery use daily as a complement to their sitting meditation practice.

Chapter 5: Sikhism

Gilbar, Steve, and Parmatma Singh. *Guru for the Aquarian Age: The Life and Teachings of Guru Nanak*. Santa Cruz, NM: Yogiji Press, 1996.

> This compilation summarizes the biography of the first Sikh guru, along with several narratives by him. It highlights the Muslim and Hindu influences on his meditations on God.

Chapter 6: Confucianism

Neville, Robert C. *Boston Confucianism: Portable Tradition in the Late-Modern World*. New York: State University of New York Press, 2000.

> Neville invites Western readers to reclaim traditions and rituals necessary to thrive in a postmodern world. This book integrates popular culture with a scholarly examination of Confucian philosophy and its potential for Christian dialogue.

Wei-Ming, Tu. *Humanity and Self-Cultivation*. Boston: Cheng and Tsui, 1999.

> This work from the established neo-Confucian scholar Tu Wei-Ming analyzes the spiritual dimension of this tradition and its meaning for a global community.

Chapter 7: Taoism

Hoff, Benjamin. *The Tao of Pooh*. New York: Penguin, 1983.

> This classic novel compares Pooh-bear, his friends, and their respective Taoist values. In this engaging modern tale, Hoff contends that simplicity and natural living embody the teachings of Lao-Tzu.

Ming-Dao, Deng. *365 Tao: Daily Meditations*. New York: HarperCollins, 1992.

> This concise book supplies daily reflections on Taoist aphorisms that provide a positive method for cultivating internal calm and focus.

Chapter 8: Shinto

Last Samurai, The. Warner Home Video, 2003 (154 minutes, rated R).

> This film looks at the period of Japanese history in which the *bushido*, or warrior class, faced extinction from modernization during the 1870s. It is rated R for violence, but explains how honor and pride permeate the Shinto tradition. For the viewers who are minors, obtain parental permission to view an R-rated movie, and use your best judgment about the appropriateness of the film and the advisability of viewing relevant excerpts.

Ono, Sokyo. *Shinto: The Kami Way*. North Clarendon, VT: Tuttle, 1962.

> This classic Shinto overview discusses the ways the Eastern faith tradition of *kami* influences Japanese architecture, festivals, and worship. It emphasizes *kami*'s communal dimension.

Chapter 9: Judaism

Heschel, Abraham Joshua. *I Asked for Wonder: A Spiritual Anthology*. Edited by Samuel H. Dresner. New York: Crossroad, 1998.

> This collection of prayers and reflections from the twentieth-century rabbi provides an insight into the spiritual vision of a great Jewish mystic and social reformer.

Neusner, Jacob. *Children of the Flesh, Children of the Promise: A Rabbi Talks with Paul*. Cleveland: The Pilgrim Press, 1995.

> This comparative work highlights the need for tolerance and understanding among the monotheistic traditions. It also creates a figurative conversation between contemporary and historical Judaism.

Wylen, Stephen M. *Setting of Silver: An Introduction to Judaism*. Mahwah, NJ: Paulist Press, 1989.

> Wylen summarizes the central beliefs and rituals of Judaism in this comprehensive introduction. It includes an examination of modern influences on Judaism's historical practices.

Chapter 10: Christianity

Empires: Peter and Paul and the Christian Revolution. PBS Home Video, 2003 (120 minutes, not rated).

> This historical documentary traces the origins of Christianity through political conflict and religious persecution. It contains interviews with various scholars and reenactments of key events in its early years of evangelization.

Tillich, Paul. *A History of Christian Thought: From Its Judaic and Hellenistic Origins to Existentialism*. New York: Simon and Schuster, 1967.

> This systematic treatment of the history of Christianity focuses on cultural and philosophical influences on its doctrine. Tillich's work remains one of the authoritative sources on Christian theology.

Chapter 11: Islam

Caner, Ergun Mehmet, and Emir Fethi Caner. *Unveiling Islam: An Insider's Look at Muslim Life and Beliefs*. Grand Rapids, MI: Kregel, 2002.

This bestselling book presents a firsthand account of Islam and how its beliefs and ideals have been seen in a post–9-11 world. In particular it highlights the similarities with Christianity by examining Islamic and Christian Scriptures and media portrayals.

Inside Mecca. National Geographic, 2003 (60 minutes, not rated).

This documentary looks at the annual pilgrimage to Mecca and sheds light on the universal principles of Islam during the days of the *Hajj*. It follows the personal stories of the pilgrims and the mental preparation, physical strain, and spiritual ecstasy they encounter on their journeys.

Chapter 12: A World of Perspectives

Eck, Diana. *A New Pluralism of America: How a "Christian Country" Has Become One of the World's Most Religious Nations*. New York: HarperCollins, 2001.

Eck presents an overview of the architecture and practices of religious groups across the United States. She contends that Christianity now stands as one among many traditions.

Faith and Reason. 7 vols. PBS Home Video, 2007 (60 minutes each, not rated).

Bill Moyers explores the issue of tolerance with leading thinkers by looking at the relationship between religious fundamentalism and democracy, equality, and human rights.

Knitter, Paul. *No Other Name? A Critical Survey of Christian Attitudes Toward the World Religions*. Maryknoll, NY: Orbis, 1985.

Knitter evaluates several models for relating world religions to one another. He recognizes that authentic dialogue is challenging and requires an interpretation of what constitutes uniqueness in the Christian tradition.

Acknowledgments

The excerpt on page 6 is from *Dialogue and Proclamation: Reflection and Orientations on Interreligious Dialogue and the Proclamation of the Gospel of Jesus Christ,* by the Pontifical Council for Inter-Religious Dialogue, number 14, at *www.vatican.va/roman_curia/pontifical_councils/interelg/documents/rc_pc_interelg_doc_19051991_dialogue-and-proclamatio_en.html,* accessed October 13, 2008.

The sermon on handout 1–A is from *The Intrareligious Dialogue,* revised edition, by Raimon Panikkar (Mahwah, NJ: Paulist Press, 1999), page 1. Copyright © 1999 by Raimon Panikkar. Used with permission of Paulist Press, Inc., *www.paulistpress.com.*

The prayer on handout 2–B is from *Black Elk: Holy Man of the Oglala,* by Michael F. Steltenkamp (Norman, OK: University of Oklahoma Press, 1993), pages 118–119. Copyright © 1993 by the University of Oklahoma Press. Used with permission of the University of Oklahoma Press.

The excerpts on handout 3–C are from *Divine Mother, Blessed Mother: Hindu Goddesses and the Virgin Mary,* by Francis X. Clooney (New York: Oxford University Press, 2005), pages 51, 52, 53, 54, 55, 66, 67, and 68, respectively. Copyright © 2005 by Oxford University Press. Used with permission of Oxford University Press.

The Sikh wedding hymn on handout 5–C is from *The Name of My Beloved: Verses of the Sikh Gurus,* translated by Nikky-Guninder Kaur Singh (New York: HarperCollins Publishers, 1995), pages 147–148. Copyright © 1995 by Nikky-Guninder Kaur Singh. Used with permission of the author.

The quotation on page 43 is from *Confucius: The Secular as Sacred,* by Herbert Fingarette (New York: Harper and Row Publishers, 1972), page 75. Copyright © 1972 by Herbert Fingarette.

The material on handout 6–B is from *The Doctrine of the Mean,* by Confucius, translated by James Legge (Oxford, England: Clarendon Press, 1893), at *www.sacred-texts.com/cfu/conf3.htm,* accessed October 13, 2008.

The material on handout 6–C is from *Chinese Civilization: A Sourcebook,* second edition, revised, edited by Patricia Buckley Ebrey (New York: The Free Press, a division of Macmillan, 1993), page 24. Copyright © 1993 by Patricia Buckley Ebrey. Reprinted with permission of The Free Press, a division of Simon and Schuster, Inc.

The quotation on page 50 is from *The Taoist Body,* by Kristofer Schipper, translated by Karen C. Duval (Berkeley, CA: University of California Press, 1993), page 2. Copyright © 1993 by the Regents of the University of California.

The excerpt on page 57 is from *A Sand County Almanac, and Sketches Here and There,* by Aldo Leopold (New York: Oxford University Press, 1987), page 204. Copyright © 1949 by Oxford University Press.

The prayer on page 58 is from *Norito: A Translation of the Ancient Japanese Ritual Prayers,* by Donald L. Philippi (Princeton, NJ: Princeton University Press, 1990), page 59. Copyright © 1991 by Princeton University Press. Used with permission of Princeton University Press.

The quotation on handout 8–A is from *Motoori Norinaga Zensh,* by Motoori Norinaga (Tokyo, 1901), as quoted in *The National Faith of Japan: A Study in Modern Shinto,* by D. C. Holtom (New York: Paragon Book Reprint Corp., 1965), page 23.

The material on handout 9–B is from *The Wisdom of Heschel,* selected by Ruth Marcus Goodhill (New York: Farrar, Straus and Giroux, 1975), pages 205–209. Copyright © 1970, 1972, 1975 by Sylvia Heschel, Executrix of the Estate of Abraham Joshua Heschel. Used with permission.